Housing Markets and Congressional Goals

Ernest M. Fisher

The Praeger Special Studies program—utilizing the most modern and efficient book production techniques and a selective worldwide distribution network—makes available to the academic, government, and business communities significant, timely research in U.S. and international economic, social, and political development.

Housing Markets and Congressional Goals

PRAEGER SPECIAL STUDIES IN U.S. ECONOMIC, SOCIAL, AND POLITICAL ISSUES

Praeger Publishers   New York   Washington   London

Library of Congress Cataloging in Publication Data

Fisher, Ernest McKinley, 1893-
    Housing markets and congressional goals.

    (Praeger special studies in U.S. economic, social,
and political issues)
    1. Housing—United States.   2. Housing subsidies—
United States.   I. Title.
HD7293.F562   301.5'4'0973   74-9423
ISBN 0-275-09950-4

PRAEGER PUBLISHERS
111 Fourth Avenue, New York, N.Y. 10003, U.S.A.
5, Cromwell Place, London SW7 2JL, England

Published in the United States of America in 1975
by Praeger Publishers, Inc.

Printed in the United States of America

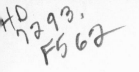

This book consists of comments on the provisions in
the Housing and Development Act of 1968, in which the
Congress "affirms" and "reaffirms" the "National goal, as
set forth in Section 2 of the Housing Act of 1949, of 'a
decent home and a suitable environment for every American
family,'" and "finds that this goal has not been fully
realized for many of the Nation's lower income families;
that this is a matter of grave national concern; . . .
[and] determines that it can be substantially achieved
within the next decade by the construction of rehabilitation of twenty-six million housing units, six million of
these for low and moderate income families."[1]

This act was remarkable not only for containing these
affirmations, reaffirmations, and findings, but also for
its size; it covers 136 pages, and contains, according to
the Report of the Chairman to the House Banking and Currency Committee, 16 "major features." Said the Chairman
in this report:

> For the first time we have a program of
> direct Government aid to make homeownership
> possible for families who could not other-
> wise afford decent homes of their own.
> Homeownership, long recognized as a basic
> part of the American way of life, has a
> significance that goes beyond housing alone.
> The sense of dignity, pride, and responsi-
> bility is a value beyond calculation.
>
> The many other new features of the bill
> include assistance in the creation of new
> communities which in the long run will serve
> to relieve population pressures on our over-
> crowded cities, protection for the consumer
> from misrepresentation of land sold in in-
> terstate commerce, a new approach to financ-
> ing college housing at charges which the
> average student can afford, a new program
> to aid self-help housing in small towns and
> rural areas, a new approach to urban renewal
> which will accelerate progress and at the
> same time enable cities to undertake more
> comprehensive programs, Federal assistance

to assure that every property owner can obtain the insurance protection he needs, and
the creation of the long-sought program of
flood insurance.

In addition, the act provides substantial additional financing for the existing
programs of low-rent public housing, model
cities, urban renewal, water and sewer
grants, and for other programs.[2]

Other provisions of the Act and its legislative history make it clear that the Congress was prepared to support its findings and to adopt the recommendations of the
Executive, to be calculated in a report required of the
Executive each year, for legislation and appropriations
necessary to enable achievement of the goal within the
decade contemplated.

My interest in this extraordinary piece of legislation was first aroused by receipt of a request to advise
or consult on some of the problems that might arise in the
process of trying to achieve this quota of the Congress.
The more I studied the Act and its history, and the history of the active intervention of our Federal government
in housing markets, the more I came to question both the
means suggested in the Act for accomplishing the goal, and
the process of analysis by which the numbers incorporated
into the Act were arrived at by both the Congress and those
who had important influence in getting Congressional adoption of both the process and the numbers.

Having participated in the drafting and adoption of
rules and regulations establishing the program of the
Federal Housing Administration in 1934, and having assisted one of the principal proponents of the National
Housing Act of 1937 on the floor of the Senate when the
Act was being debated; and having prepared in 1960 at
the request of the Administrator of the Housing and Home
Finance Agency a critique of the then current housing programs and policies of the Federal government, I found myself obliged to satisfy my intellectual curiosity about
the trends in governmental intervention in housing markets
by making a study of this Act.

Since I had divested myself of most of the advisory
work for which I had assumed responsibility since retiring
from the faculty of Columbia University, I decided to review, in connection with this study, the materials on
housing markets in the United States and Western European
countries that I had collected over a period of some forty

years, and analyze the provisions of the Act of 1968 in the light of these materials as well as of my own personal experience. I have given special attention to the invaluable materials on domestic housing that the Bureau of the Census has been producing and improving in both content and coverage over these decades, much of which I have been closely connected with.

After this study, I found it difficult to accept either the reasoning or the production quota represented in this Act.

This work has been entirely gratuitous on my part, and sometimes rather laborious, since I have no secretarial, stenographic, statistical-clerical, or computer assistance, except what I employ at my own expense. But it has served the excellent purpose of keeping my mind occupied with thoughts other than those centered on the process of growing old. (This is a valuable service; as has been said of a dog's having fleas: it keeps him from thinking too much about the fact that he is a dog).

The more materials I studied, the more I became convinced that the numbers were unrealistic as a quota of production, and that as a means of achieving the "affirmed" and "reaffirmed" goal of the Congress, they were inappropriate and would probably prove as disappointing as had many of the programs presented to and adopted by the Congress over the past two and a half decades.

These conclusions have not been reached easily or thoughtlessly. They have not led me to renounce or even to question seriously the conviction I came to early in my study of housing markets, while a member of the faculty of the University of Michigan; namely, that governments must play a much more active part than in the past in abolishing the shameful conditions in which a large portion of the adults and children of the industrialized societies of Western Europe and the United States are housed.

But they have convinced me that much more thought must be given to the means these governments employ in trying to realize the gleaming goal of "a decent home and a suitable environment" for all their citizens.

If this book promotes the type of study and statistical analysis that leads to the adoption by our Congress of more appropriate and effective means of achieving its official goal, the work and expense involved in its preparation will have been more than adequately compensated.

NOTES

1. Housing and Urban Development Act of 1968 (Public Law 90-448, 90th Congress, S. 3497, August 1, 1968; 82 Stat. 476).

2. "Letter of Transmittal" of "Compilation of the Housing and Urban Development Act of 1968" to the Committee on Banking and Currency of the House of Representatives, 90th Congress, Second Session (Washington, D.C.: Government Printing Office, 1968).

CONTENTS

		Page
PREFACE		v
LIST OF TABLES		xi

Chapter

1 ORIGINS OF A CONGRESSIONAL "QUOTA" FOR CONSTRUCTION — 1

   Notes — 24

2 STANDING STOCK AS AN "ADEQUATE HOUSING" RESOURCE — 26

   Notes — 33

3 THE ROLE OF "USED" AND NEW HOUSING IN SERVING LOW- AND MIDDLE-INCOME HOUSEHOLDS — 35

   Legislation Promoting New Housing — 37
   New Homes Are for Incremental Demand — 38
   Notes — 45

4 ELIMINATION OF "SUBSTANDARD" HOUSING UNITS — 47

   Notes — 54

5 BUILDING TO INCREASE VACANCIES? — 58

   Notes — 69

6 DELINQUENCIES, FORECLOSURES, AND UNSOLD INVENTORY — 71

   Notes — 84

7 OVERCROWDING AND THE "NEED" FOR SECOND HOMES — 85

   Notes — 90

Chapter   Page

   8   CRITIQUE OF PROJECTIONS   91

       The Error of Aggregate Projections   92
       Capital Versus Occupancy Costs   103
       Notes   115

   9   PROGRESS TOWARD THE "GOAL"   121

       Notes   134

  10   NEEDED CHANGES IN FEDERAL HOUSING PROGRAMS   135

       Notes   148

ABOUT THE AUTHOR   149

LIST OF TABLES

Table   Page

1.1   Estimated Total Number of Housing Units
        and Number of Privately Owned Housing
        Units Started in the United States
        Annually, 1950-73   3

1.2   Amount and Percentage Increase in the
        Boeckh Index of Residential Construction
        Costs, of the Average Sale Prices of New
        Homes Purchased with the Assistance of
        an FHA-Insured Mortgage, and of the
        Bureau of the Census' Index of Prices of
        New Homes over Selected Time Periods   9

1.3   Numerical and Percentage Increase of
        Nonfarm Population, of Nonfarm Housing
        Units in the Inventory, and of Nonfarm
        Households, with Estimates of the
        Number of Nonfarm Housing Starts, by
        Decades, 1920-70   12

1.4   Total Population of the United States,
        Total Urban Population 1790 to 1910;
        Total Nonfarm Population (Urban and
        Rural Nonfarm) 1920-70; and Numerical
        and Percentage Increases During
        Intercensal Periods   14

1.5   Numerical and Percentage Increase in
        Nonfarm Housing Units, and in Nonfarm
        Households; and Estimated Number of
        Nonfarm Housing Starts, by Decades
        1890-1970   15

1.6   Total Population, Number of Families,
        Number of Households, with Average
        Number of Persons per Household and
        per Family, in the United States
        1940, 1950, 1960, and 1970, and with
        Numerical and Percentage Increases
        During Intercensal Periods   16

1.7a   Selected Population Projections of the
        Bureau of the Census   18

xi

Table   Page

1.7b   Increase in Population Indicated by
        Population Projections of the Bureau
        of the Census   19

1.8   Numerical and Percentage Distribution of
        Households in the United States, by
        Number of Persons, 1940, 1950, 1960,
        and 1970, with Numerical and Percentage
        Increases During Intercensal Periods   20

2.1   Numerical and Percentage Distribution in
        1960 and 1970 of Owner-Occupied and
        "Vacant for Sale" Housing Units by Value
        Classes and of Single-Family Units Sold,
        1963-70, by Price Classes   28

2.2   Percentage Distribution of Home Owners in
        1970, by Income Classes and Numerical
        and Percentage Distribution of Purchasers
        of New and Previously Occupied Homes
        During 1969, by Income Classes   30

2.3   Numerical and Percentage Distribution of
        Housing Units Rented and for Rent and
        of Units in Apartment Houses Built and
        Rented in 1970, by Monthly Rent   31

2.4   Number of Homes Bought for Owner Occupancy
        by Years, with Percentage Consisting of
        Previously Occupied Units   31

3.1   U.S. Bureau of the Census Projections of
        Number of Households in the United
        States at Selected Dates   41

3.2   Increases in Population from 1970 to 1980
        (or 1975 to 1980) Suggested by the
        Projections of the U.S. Bureau of the
        Census Made in 1960, 1969, and 1972, with
        the Ratio of These Projected Increases
        to the Number of New Dwelling Units
        Proposed to be Constructed in Accordance
        with the Provisions of the Act of 1968   42

Table   Page

3.3   Estimated U.S. Farm Population, 1950 to
       1972, with Annual Numerical Decrease
       (or Increase) for Selected Terms of Years   44

4.1   Estimated Annual Expenditure of Owners of
       Residential Units and of Owner-Occupants
       of Single-Family Units for Additions,
       Alterations, Maintenance and Repairs,
       and Replacements; and Estimates of Total
       Purchase Price Paid by Purchasers of New
       Single-Family Homes for Selected Years   53

5.1   Estimated Total Nonfarm Housing Inventory,
       Number of Units Occupied and Percentage
       Unoccupied at Census Dates 1890, 1900,
       1910, 1920, 1930, 1940, 1950, 1960, and
       1970; with Total Number Classified as
       "Urban" and "Inside SMSA's," with Number
       Occupied and Percentage Not Occupied at
       the Census Dates 1950, 1960, and 1970   61

5.2   Estimated Vacancy and Occupancy Rates for
       Housing Units at Selected Dates   63

5.3   Estimated Length of Tenure of All Reporting
       Households and of Owner-Occupants and
       Renters in 1970   66

6.1   Number and Rate of Foreclosure of Nonfarm
       Mortgages and of Mortgages in the
       Portfolios of Insured Savings and Loan
       Associations, 1946-73   73

6.2   Number and Rate of Delinquencies at Year
       End of FHA-Insured Home Mortgages,
       1950-73   75

6.3   Percentage of One-to-Four-Family Mortgage
       Loans Serviced by Members of MBA
       Reported in Default at Selected Year
       Ends by Type of Mortgage   77

6.4   Number of FHA- and VA-Insured or Guaran-
       teed Home Mortgages Foreclosed (or Deed
       in Lieu Received) by Years, 1950-72,
       with Foreclosure Rate   80

xiii

Table   Page

6.5   Mortgage Delinquency Rates, Reported by
       Life Insurance Companies on Selected
       Types of Mortgage Investments   81

6.6   Ratio of the Number of New Homes "For
       Sale" at the End of the Year to the
       Total Number Sold During the Year,
       1963-73   82

7.1   Numerical and Percentage Distribution of
       Occupied Housing Units in the United
       States in 1970 by Number of Persons per
       Room and by Tenure   86

7.2   Numerical and Percentage Distribution of
       Housing Units by Number of Rooms and of
       Households by Number of Persons, 1970   87

8.1   Percentage of Gain or Loss in Population
       1950 to 1960 and 1960 to 1970 for
       Selected SMSA's   95

8.2   Selected SMSA's in Which Maximum Loss and
       Maximum Gains in Population Were
       Reported for Smaller Statistical Areas
       in the Same SMSA   96

8.3   Number of Standard Metropolitan Statis-
       tical Areas Having Minimum and Maximum
       Percentage of Growth in Population by
       Migration, 1960-70, by Population Size
       Groups, with the Numbers and Rate of
       Gain or Loss   102

8.4   Percentage of New One-Family Homes Sold
       While Under Construction or Before
       Started at the End of the Month of
       Sale, March, June, and September,
       1970-73   106

8.5   The Number of Starts of New Housing Units
       Reported in the Fourth Annual Report,
       Achieved During the Years 1969-72;
       Targeted Number Scheduled in the Second
       Annual Report for the Years 1973-78,
       with Number and Percentage of Total
       Unsubsidized and Subsidized   109

xiv

Table   Page

9.1   Projections of Volume of Subsidized,
       Unsubsidized, Rehabilitated, and
       Mobile Units to be Produced Each Year
       in the Decade 1968-78 in the First
       and Second Annual Reports of the
       President on National Housing Goals   125

10.1   Increase in Numbers of Housing Units on
       Which Subsidy Payments Were Made or
       Were Committed, or on Which Such
       Payments Were Anticipated in Budget
       Requests for the Fiscal Years, 1971,
       1972, and 1973   137

Housing Markets and Congressional Goals

1

ORIGINS OF A
CONGRESSIONAL "QUOTA"
FOR CONSTRUCTION

The Bureau of the Census reports that the Census of Housing of 1970 counted 68.7 million housing units in the housing stock. This was just over 10.3 million or 18 percent more than were counted in the Census of 1960.

During the decade of the 1950s, the increase was more than 15 million. Just over 14 million were built during the 1960s. That is, during the two decades, 1950 to 1969, 30 million new units were built. This is a record that had never been approached during any two decades of our history. The number of units produced during this 20-year stretch was equal to just about 65 percent of the number available at the beginning of the period; and over 80 percent of the total number, 37 million, in the inventory in 1940.

But among the members of the Congress, the officers of the Department of Housing and Urban Development (HUD), and many other concerned observers, this record had not gone very far in meeting what has become labeled the nation's "housing needs."

In 1968, legislation was enacted which read:

> The Congress finds that the supply of
> the Nation's housing is not increasing
> rapidly enough to meet the national hous-
> ing goal, established in the Housing Act
> of 1949, of the "realization as soon as
> feasible of a decent home and a suitable
> environment for every American family."
> The Congress reaffirms this national
> housing goal and determines that it can
> be substantially achieved within the

1

next decade by the construction or rehabilitation of twenty-six million housing
units, six million of these for low and
moderate income families.[1]

This is the first time in history that the Congress
ever specified the number of housing units that should be
constructed or reconstructed within a designated period
of time. How the number should be distributed over the
years of the decade was not indicated; but it is not a
difficult mathematical exercise to determine that, however distributed, an annual average production of approximately 2.6 million units would be required, of which 2
million units would be newly built.

The largest number of new units started in any year
prior to 1968 was a little over 1.6 million recorded in
1955 and 1963 (see Table 1.1).*

During the three years following each of these peaks,
starts averaged nearly 1.4 million units a year. The
first year after the peak of 1955, 1.3 million units were
started; and by 1966, the third year after the 1963 peak,
starts fell to a little more than 1.1 million units.

During the decade 1950 to 1960 more than 15 million
new units were started, and it is reasonable to suppose
that approximately that number had been completed and
added to the nonfarm inventory, which in 1950, according
to the Census of Housing made in that year, numbered 39.6
million units; and in 1970, the nonfarm inventory numbered some 68.7 million units, an increase during the two
decades of 29 million, or about 74 percent.

It was quite generally realized at the beginning of
this period that with the migrations during and following
World War II, and with the return of the members of the
armed forces to civilian status, the urban housing inventory was very densely occupied. Even during the war, rent

---

*These numbers represent the estimates of starts, not
completions. The official estimates of number of starts
indicate that in 1950 the total was 1.9 million. But this
number must be taken with a grain of salt. Announcement
in the late fall of 1950 of the imposition of restraints
of credit extended for units "not under construction" at
a given future date, when the restrictions would become
effective, caused a rush to "dig a hole and get in under
the wire." How many of these starts resulted in completed structures during the following year has not been
recorded.

TABLE 1.1

Estimated Total Number of Housing Units and Number
of Privately Owned Housing Units Started in the
United States Annually, 1950-73
(in thousands)

Year	Total	Privately Owned
1950	1,952	1,908
1951	1,491	1,420
1952	1,504	1,446
1953	1,438	1,402
1954	1,551	1,532
1955	1,646	1,627
1956	1,349	1,325
1957	1,224	1,175
1958	1,382	1,314
1959	1,553.5[a]	1,494.6[b]
1960	1,296.0	1,230.1
1961	1,365.0	1,284.8
1962	1,491.4	1,439.1
1963	1,640.9	1,581.7
1964	1,590.8	1,530.4
1965	1,509.6	1,472.9[c]
1966	1,195.9	1,472.9
1967	1,321.9	1,291.6
1968	1,545.5	1,507.7
1969	1,499.6	1,466.8
1970	1,469.0	1,433.6
1971	2,083.2	1,500.8
1972	2,376.8	2,354.9
1973	2,057.4	2,045.2

[a]From 1959 includes "farm."

[b]From 1959 to 1964, excludes "farm."

[c]From 1965, includes "farm."

Source: Domestic and International Business Administration, Bureau of Domestic Commerce, U.S. Department
of Commerce, Construction Review, selected issues.

3

control had been instituted to prevent skyrocketing rents; and materials for construction were rationed and allowed to be used only in those communities where war materials and supplies were being produced, or other military activities were being carried on.

It was in November 1944 that the first official estimate was made of the volume of residential construction necessary to overcome the shortages that these circumstances had produced. At that time, the Administrator of the National Housing Agency indicated that

> to provide for population and family increases and to start making up past deficiencies . . . during the first 10 years after the war, a total of 12.6 million non-farm dwelling units will be needed. . . . About half the need will be new need, originating in the increase in the number of families; the remainder is replacement need.[2]

In the detailed calculations, the increase in the number of families was estimated at 6.2 million during the first decade after the close of the war; hence 6.3 million units would be required "to bring the total number of vacancies up to 5 percent of total supply"; and 6.3 million new units would be required to replace "units destroyed by fire, storm, and flood," and "substandard units demolished."[3]

This bulletin set the pattern for official estimates, which followed each other at irregular intervals for 24 years, culminating in the Congressional dictate of 26 million units to be built new or rehabilitated during the decade 1968-78.

The next official estimate was made by the Joint Congressional Committee on Housing in 1948.[4] This estimate indicated that for 12 years, 1948 to 1960, an annual volume of "between 1.3 million and 1.5 million nonfarm units" or a total between 15.6 and 18.0 million would be needed.

In commenting on this estimate, the Housing and Home Finance Administration (HHFA) Administrator, in his report for the year 1958, made the following observation:

> The Joint Committee report is cast in terms of the social needs for housing. Thus more than half of the twelve-year

> requirements are to replace substandard
> and otherwise inadequate housing. . . .
> Most of the estimates [of housing needs]
> which are below the Joint Committee's
> total have been calculated in terms of
> market demand rather than social needs.[5]

Thus the dichotomy of social need and market demand become established in official gobbledygook and the implicit tenet of both the Congress and the administrations that a part of annual production should be intended for and made available to households in all income ranges was made explicit and seems thenceforth to have pervaded their thinking and actions.

There was no other official estimate of the volume of residential building necessary until 1960. In April of that year, the subcommittee on housing of the Senate Committee on Banking and Currency, after extensive hearings, reported to the Committee that "the subcommittee believes that a minimum of 16 million permanent nonfarm housing units should be constructed during the ten year period beginning in January, 1961."[6]

No reference was made to where these 16 million new units should be built, except by noticing that the need for new units was not going to be uniform throughout the country or even over a whole metropolitan area: "Migration from one region to another and a continuation of the strong movement to the suburbs will certainly continue in the 1960's and will require substantial numbers of new units to house those families moving into housing shortage areas."[7]

There was also scant reference to the price ranges into which these 16 million new houses should be distributed. Attention was called to the current and probable future distribution of personal income, and it was indicated that "(1) relatively more families will have incomes sufficient to afford decent housing, and (2) there will be a substantial increase in the quality of the homes that American families can afford."[8]

Great emphasis was placed upon the role of credit in stimulating new home building, and upon the use of liberal financing terms in making the new homes available to those prospective purchasers who were unable to meet down payment requirements and to qualify as likely to be able to meet periodic mortgage debt service.

There seems to be no reference in the subcommittee's report to the influence of credit terms upon builders' prices, save a long quotation from a paper prepared for the subcommittee by Mr. Ramsey Wood. The pertinent passage quoted from that paper pointed out that

> making credit available on easier terms
> is not analogous to giving everyone a cash
> gift, for example, or to reducing the
> prices of houses. On the contrary, easier
> terms give an immediate advantage to only
> some bidders, and will usually result in
> higher prices than would prevail under
> less liberal terms.
> . . . With any given composition of
> demand and of supply, the credit terms
> available largely determine the level of
> values for the standing stock of houses.[9]

In conclusion, the subcommittee observed:

> Existing law gives considerable discretion
> to administrative agencies of the Federal
> Government to cause changes in credit
> terms for transactions in residential real
> estate. The principles related in the
> summary by Mr. Ramsay Wood are generally
> sound and are recommended to the careful
> attention of Federal agencies which have
> this discretion.[10]

But in the final summary of recommendations, Recommendation No. 9 stated plainly that

> the subcommittee believes that the na-
> tional housing policy of a decent home
> and suitable living environment for
> every American family cannot be achieved
> within the forseeable future without the
> creation of new programs designed to solve
> this problem. Consequently, the subcom-
> mittee recommends that bills now pending
> which propose a Federal program to in-
> crease the volume of residential construc-
> tion for middle-income families, should
> be given high priority and should be con-
> sidered as soon as possible during [the]
> current session of Congress.[11]

This conclusion followed the tentative one which was placed at the end of several pages of discussion of the hearings on "Middle-Income Housing." It stated:

> Existing institutions available to help achieve the national housing policy . . . are inadequate. It is evident that families of low and moderate income cannot be housed decently, within the foreseeable future, unless new programs for this purpose are fostered by the Federal Government, or by State and local governments, or by all levels of government.[12]

One other topic that received considerable attention in this report and in the hearings that preceded it was "the stabilization of the home building industry." Recommendation No. 5 reads:

> The subcommittee believes that the instability of residential construction, which is partially attributable to monetary policy, should be minimized, [and it was added that the Federal Reserve Board should be requested to make a report] not later than January 1, 1961, which report shall . . . include . . . an analysis of residential construction activity during the period 1946 through 1959. . . . An explanation of the factors which have contributed to instability in residential construction during this period . . . [and] recommendations for minimizing this instability during the ten-year period beginning in January 1961, recognizing the need for a minimum construction of 16 million permanent nonfarm units and recognizing the need for general economic growth and stability.[13]

The actions of the Administration during the year 1960, as reported in the Annual Report, indicated that all the admonitions of this subcommittee report had been taken seriously, except the one that recommended that the principles related in the summary by Mr. Ramsey Wood be given careful attention. Notwithstanding the concern expressed in Mr. Wood's paper that "making credit

available on easier terms . . . will usually result in
higher prices than would prevail under less liberal terms,"
in January the Federal National Mortgage Association (FNMA)
increased the maximum amount of an insured or guaranteed
mortgage eligible for sale to it under its secondary market program from $15,000 to $20,000; and on April 29, the
Federal Housing Administration (FHA) reduced the down-
payment requirements in its program to 3 percent of $13,500
of appraised value, plus 10 percent of the next $4,500 of
value, plus 30 percent of value above $18,000, which was
within its "discretion."

Thus it was made possible for a purchaser using an
FHA insured mortgage to buy a $13,500 house by making a
down payment of $405; a $20,000 house by making a down
payment of $1,455; and a $25,000 house with a down payment
of $1,605. And the price of both new and existing houses
that were purchased during 1961 with the assistance of an
FHA insured mortgage increased by 1.58 and 2.60 percent,
respectively, while the Boeckh index of cost of residential construction increased by a little less than three-
tenths of 1 percent (see Table 1.2).

Both reports expanded the list of sources of need;
to the three previously recognized sources, of "new families" (by which apparently is meant additional households), the replacement of "substandard and otherwise inadequate housing," and "units needed to build up the
vacancy ratio to a more normal level," were added the
items of (1) migration and mobility of established families (again probably meaning households); (2) "the needs
of minority groups"; (3) the needs of "the aging"; and
(4) units needed to replace those dropped from the inventory because of "destruction, demolition, or abandonment
or conversion."

> To achieve these goals [the report con-
> tinued] calls for special aids for moder-
> ate income families [again, probably mean-
> ing households] for an expanded and re-
> vitalized low-rent public housing program,
> an expanded program of housing for the
> elderly, and for more effective aids to
> residential rehabilitation and conserva-
> tion. . . .[14]

In this report of the HHFA the first reference is
found to two phenomena of importance in judging the
soundness of private housing markets:

TABLE 1.2

Amount and Percentage Increase in the Boeckh Index of Residential Construction
Costs, of the Average Sale Prices of New Homes Purchased with the Assistance
of an FHA-Insured Mortgage, and of the Bureau of the Census' Index of
Prices of New Homes over Selected Time Periods
(in percents unless otherwise indicated)

Time Period	Boeckh Index		Sale Prices of New Homes		Bureau of Census New Home Price Index	
	Index	Increase	Amount (in dollars)	Increase	Index	Increase
1955-60	11.8	12.7	$2,549	21.0	NA	NA
1960-65	11.0	10.5	2,163	14.7	NA	NA
1963-65	6.7	6.1	1,036	6.5	0.3	3.2
1966-71	38.5	40.8	6,230	35.3	.31	32.9
1968-71	25.5	23.7	4,267	21.8	.19	17.9

Sources: Calculated from Construction Review, HUD Statistical Yearbooks, and
Bureau of the Census, Construction Reports, C20-71-6, August 1971.

In the second quarter of 1960, the proportions of all units in the housing inventory that were vacant, . . . advanced to 3.5 percent and remained at that figure to the end of the year. This was the highest rate in the postwar period, and was appreciably higher than the 3.0 percent prevailing in the second half of 1959. . . . The rental vacancy rate was 7.6 percent at the end of the year.[15]

The second item to which strange reference was made was the report of a rising foreclosure rate:

The estimated number of nonfarm real estate foreclosures [apparently referring to real estate mortgage foreclosures] in 1960 was about 50,000, a 14 percent increase over 1959. This rate of change was markedly greater than the 4 percent increase between 1958 and 1959. The high [sic!] number of foreclosures also resulted in measurable increase in the rate of foreclosure per 1000 mortgaged residential units. . . . This rate rose to 2.66, . . . the highest rate in 11 years for which comparable data are available, but was still well below what a comparable rate would have been in the early thirties when foreclosures ran to about 250,000 per year. [Emphasis added.][16]

As a matter of fact, the two Federal mortgage insurance or guarantee agencies, the FHA and the Veterans Administration (VA), encountered an increasing volume and rate of foreclosures from 1957 and 1958 to 1965. Further attention to this phenomenon will be given later.

No specific reference is made to these phenomena in the recommendation of a construction quota of 1.6 million new units a year to be attained in the very near future and 2 million units by the end of the decade. This report shifted the emphasis from sheer volume to numbers "needed" in the price ranges and for those fragments of the total market to which the Administration wanted to direct attention.

The most surprising aspect of both of these reports is their failure to observe and interpret the changes that had been brought about in housing markets between 1945--the end of the war--and the date of the projections. As a matter of fact, the interpretation of the statistical materials considered followed very closely the pattern established by the National Housing Administrator in 1943.

While the record production of the decade of the 1950s of 15 million nonfarm units--about a third as many as existed at the beginning--had not yet been completed, it was near enough to the end of the decade to assure that such a record-breaking volume was certain to be realized. And the record was not only in the number of units produced, but also in the percentage increase of the inventory. The total nonfarm inventory increase of 38 percent exceeded that of any decade for which there is an acceptable record, except that following World War I, 1920 to 1930, when the only records we have indicate an increase that reached nearly 45 percent (see Table 1.3).

Nor should it have been unexpected that in making these projections the record of population growth during and following World War I would have been examined, since one of the bases of these projections was anticipated population growth. According to the Census reports, urban population increased from 1910 to 1920 by 29 percent; and from 1920 to 1930, by 24 percent.* And from

---

*With the growth of urban communities and of their importance in the nation, there have been some confusing changes in the terminology used in reporting population. Until after the Census of 1910, population was reported as "urban" and "rural." By the time of the Census of 1920, many homes occupied by persons who were employed in urban communities were beyond the geographic limits and the thickly settled area of cities and other urban places. In reporting population for the Census, the occupants of these places were distinguished from "farm" population, and reported as "rural nonfarm." This distinction has been maintained since, and housing units have been reported as "starts," "occupied," "unoccupied," and the like, in these categories. Hence, although the geographical area and the definition of "nonfarm" have varied from Census to Census, this terminology is used here for the sake of simplicity, to avoid confusion, and to present as accurately as possible, within the limits of a reasonable amount of adjustment, statistics that reflect the continuous and increasing importance of the ascendancy of the urban, closely settled households in the life of the nation.

TABLE 1.3

Numerical and Percentage Increase of Nonfarm Population, of Nonfarm Housing
Units in the Inventory, and of Nonfarm Households, with Estimates of the
Number of Nonfarm Housing Starts, by Decades, 1920-70

| Decade | Nonfarm Population | | Nonfarm Households | | Nonfarm Housing Units | | Nonfarm Housing Starts |
	Number	Percent	Number	Percent	Number	Percent	Number
Total	119,275	165	43,110	247	48,222	271	44,437
1920-30	18,316	24	5,700	32	7,959	44	7,004
1930-40	8,835	9	4,574	20	3,991	16	2,646
1940-50	26,273	26	9,215	29	9,942	3	5,393
1950-60	38,202	30	11,429	34	15,135	38	15,066
1960-70	27,649	17	12,192	23	11,195	20	14,326

Note: Columns may not add to totals because of rounding.

Sources: Nonfarm population figures from Statistical Abstract, 1969, p. 35; Bureau
of the Census Current Population Reports, Population Estimates and Projections, Series
25, No. 445, 1970; nonfarm households and housing units, 1920-50, Leo Grebler, Louis
Winnick, and David Blank, Capital Formation in Residential Construction (Princeton,
N.J.: Princeton University Press, for the National Bureau of Economic Research, 1955),
pp. 82, 84, 65, and appendixes F and G, pp. 387, 395; Censuses of Housing, 1950, 1960,
and 1970. The number of nonfarm households in 1970 is calculated by subtracting from
the total for the United States (63,450,000) the number (2,724,000) of farm households,
as reported by the Bureau of the Census in Current Population Reports, Population
Characteristics, "Household and Family Characteristics, 1970," Series P-20, No. 218,
March 23, 1971, p. 80. Housing Starts are from Bureau of the Census, Housing Construction Statistics, 1889-1964, p. 18; 1964-70, Bureau of the Census, Construction Reports,
"Housing Starts" includes farm housing starts.

12

1940 to 1960 the increase was by approximately the same percentage--63 percent. Thus the surge of urban or nonfarm population growth accompanying and following the two major conflicts resulted in essentially the same rate of increase.

But from 1930 to 1940 nonfarm population grew by only 9 percent. And it is not unreasonable to attribute a part of this large decline to topping out of the forces initiated by preparation for and participation in World War II.

The Subcommittee, basing its estimate upon the highest projection of the Bureau of the Census, made in 1958, assumed an increase in nonfarm population during the 1960s that paralleled that of the nearly completed 1950s--approximately 39 million (30 percent), or an average annual increase of nearly 4 million (see Table 1.4).[17]

But during the 1960s the increase in nonfarm population fell to 29 million--an increase of 17 percent, only 65 percent of the rate at which it had advanced during the 1950s. The population explosion that followed closely after World War II was "petering out."

The number of nonfarm households also continued to increase at a rapid, but declining rate--the rate of increase in the 1960s was 23 percent, as opposed to the 38 percent in the 1950s.

The average number of persons per household fell from 3.33 in 1960 to 3.17 in 1970, and the number of households consisting of only one person increased during the 1960s from 7 to 11 million. In 1970, nearly half of the 63 million households consisted of only one or two persons (see Tables 1.5 and 1.6).

It was these changes in the rate of population growth and the rate and pattern of household formation that contradicted the statement made by the HHFA in its Report of 1960:

> The decade we have just entered will be one
> of unprecedented population growth and more
> housing will have to be built than ever be-
> fore, just to keep up with it. Growing
> even now at the rate of about 3 million a
> year, population is expected to reach 214
> million by 1970.

Both the Subcommittee of the Senate Banking and Currency Committee and the HHFA had made their estimates of the need for new housing units in the light of the increase in population and in households during 1960 that

TABLE 1.4

Total Population of the United States, Total Urban Population 1790 to 1910; Total Nonfarm Population (Urban and Rural Nonfarm) 1920-70; and Numerical and Percentage Increases During Intercensal Periods
(numbers in thousands)

Census Date	Total Population Number	Increase from Previous Census Number	Percent	Nonfarm Population Number	Increase from Previous Census Number	Percent	Urban Population Number	Increase from Previous Census Number	Percent	Rural Nonfarm Population Number	Increase from Previous Census Number	Percent
1790	3,929	--	--	NA	NA	NA	202	--	--	NA	NA	NA
1800	5,308	1,379	35	NA	NA	NA	322	120	60	NA	NA	NA
1810	7,240	1,931	36	NA	NA	NA	525	203	63	NA	NA	NA
1820	9,638	2,399	33	NA	NA	NA	693	168	32	NA	NA	NA
1830	12,866	3,228	33	NA	NA	NA	1,127	434	62	NA	NA	NA
1840	17,069	4,202	33	NA	NA	NA	1,845	718	63	NA	NA	NA
1850	23,192	6,122	36	NA	NA	NA	3,544	1,699	92	NA	NA	NA
1860	31,443	8,251	36	NA	NA	NA	6,217	2,676	75	NA	NA	NA
1870	38,558	8,395	27	NA	NA	NA	9,902	3,685	59	NA	NA	NA
1880	50,189	11,631	30	NA	NA	NA	14,130	4,228	42	NA	NA	NA
1890	62,980	12,792	25	NA	NA	NA	22,106	7,976	56	NA	NA	NA
1900	76,212	13,232	21	NA	NA	NA	30,215	8,054	36	NA	NA	NA
1910	92,228	16,016	21	NA	NA	NA	42,064	11,849	39	NA	NA	NA
1920	106,022	13,794	14.9	74,317	--	--	54,253	--	--	20,164	--	--
1930	123,203	17,181	16.2	92,618	18,316	24	69,161	14,797	27	23,663	3,504	17
1940	132,165	8,962	7.2	101,453	8,835	9	74,705	5,469	7	27,129	3,366	14
1950	152,326	19,161	14.5	121,309	26,213	26	90,128	22,044	29	31,181	4,159	15
1960	179,323	27,997	18.5	163,688	36,039	28	113,056	22,929	25	50,632	19,451	62
Current Urban Definition:												
1950	151,320	19,161	14.5	127,278	--	--	96,847	--	--	30,431	--	--
1960	179,323	27,997	18.5	165,835	38,557	30	125,269	28,422	29	40,567	10,136	30
1970	203,235*	23,912	13.3	194,929	29,093	17	149,332	36,299	15	45,587	5,020	12

*Final number; items may not add to totals because of corrections and rounding.

Note: NA = Not Available.

Sources: U.S. Bureau of the Census, Census of Population 1970, "Number of Inhabitants," Final Report PC(1)-A1, "United States Summary"; U.S. Bureau of the Census and Department of Agriculture, Current Population Reports, "Farm Population in the United States, 1970," Series Census ERS, P-27,4 No. 42 (August 16, 1971).

14

TABLE 1.5

Numerical and Percentage Increase in Nonfarm Housing Units, and in Nonfarm Households; and Estimated Number of Nonfarm Housing Starts, by Decades 1890-1970

Time Period	Nonfarm Housing Units		Nonfarm Households		Nonfarm Housing Starts*
	Number	Percent	Number	Percent	Number
1890 to 1899	2,270	27.2	2,351	29.7	2,941
1900 to 1909	3,692	34.8	8,858	37.5	3,606
1910 to 1919	3,452	24.1	3,468	24.5	3,593
1920 to 1929	7,959	44.8	5,700	32.4	7,004
1930 to 1939	3,991	15.5	4,448	19.0	2,646
1940 to 1949	9,942	33.4	9,357	33.7	5,393
1950 to 1959	15,135	38.1	11,429	30.8	15,068
1960 to 1969	11,195	20.4	12,192	25.1	14,326
1920 to 1939	11,950	67.4	10,148	57.6	9,650
1940 to 1960	25,077	84.4	20,786	73.8	20,461
1950 to 1970	26,330	66.4	23,621	59.6	29,394
1920 to 1970	48,222	272.0	43,126	247.0	44,437

*Numbers in this column are taken from the following sources: From 1890 to 1949, Leo Grebler, Louis Winnick, and David Blank, Capital Formation in Residential Real Estate (Princeton, N.J.: Princeton University Press, for the National Bureau of Economic Research, 1956), p. 65; from 1950 to 1970, Bureau of the Census, Housing Starts, and Current Population Reports, Population Characteristics, "Household and Family Characteristics," March 1970, P-20, No. 218, March 23, 1971.

TABLE 1.6

Total Population, Number of Families, Number of Households, with Average Number of
Persons per Household and per Family, in the United States 1940, 1950, 1960,
and 1970, and with Numerical and Percentage Increases
During Intercensal Periods
(numbers in thousands)

	1940	1950	1960	1970
Total Resident Population	132,165	151,326	179,323	203,235
Increase from previous census:				
Number	8,962	19,161	27,997	23,912
Percent	7.2	14.5	18.5	13
Households				
Number*	34,964	42,969	53,024	62,874
Increase from previous census:				
Number	4,962	8,005	10,055	9,850
Percent	16.5	23	24	19
Number of persons	3.67	3.37	3.33	3.17
Families				
Number	32,166	39,303	45,111	51,110
Increase from previous census:				
Number	NA	4,345	5,808	5,999
Percent	NA	2.2	14	13
Number of persons	3.76	3.54	3.67	3.62

*Identical with number occupied housing units.

Sources: U.S. Bureau of the Census, Census of Housing, 1960, vol. I, part 1, "State
and Small Areas, U.S. Summary"; Current Population Reports, Population Characteristics,
"Household and Family Characteristics," March 1970, Series P-20, No. 218, March 23, 1971,
p. 79; Current Population Reports, Population Characteristics, "Selected Characteristics
of Persons and Families," March 1970.

would come if the numbers realized during that decade corresponded to those represented by the Bureau of the Census in its Series II Population Projections and its Series A projection of number of households. The Series B projection of the number of households proved to be nearest to what was realized, but the population increase from 1960 to 1970 followed more nearly the Series II projections.[18] This statement appears to have been based upon the rate of increase represented by the Series A Projection of the Bureau of the Census. But already by 1957 the increase in both the number and the rate had reached and passed their highest point, which came in both series in 1956 (when the numerical increase was estimated at 3,058,000, and the rate at 1.83 percent).[19] By 1960, according to these estimates, the numerical increase had fallen to 2,901,000, and the rate to 1.62 percent (see Tables 1.6, 1.7a, 1.7b, and 1.8).

This persistent emphasis upon the volume of new construction apparently was directed toward two objectives of both the Subcommittee and the HHFA: the first was to promote building houses for households in lower and lower income ranges, even though their occupancy would be possible only with the aid of a public subsidy; and the other was to stabilize the residential construction industry. The report of the Subcommittee gave special attention to the latter objective. And both it and the HHFA seem to have thought that it must be stabilized at a production level even higher than it had attained during the record-breaking decade of the 1950s.

In the Housing Act of 1968, the Congress gave no indication of the purposes for which the prescribed volume of construction should be intended; the Act merely states that the goal established in 1949 could be substantially achieved by the building or rehabilitation of the exact number of 26 million units during the coming decade.

The President's Committee on Urban Housing, reporting to the President on December 11, 1968, stated that:

> We have reported already, for in the months
> since you gave us this responsibility, we
> have submitted a number of recommendations
> to the White House and to the appropriate
> Departments. It was our privilege to par-
> ticipate in the development of your proposed
> omnibus housing bill this year. Whatever
> contribution we have been able to make to
> the Housing and Urban Development Act of
> 1968 [is] our response to the charge you
> gave us.[20]

TABLE 1.7a

Selected Population Projections of the Bureau of the Census
(numbers in thousands)

Date of Projection	Date to Which Projection Extends					
	1965	1970	1975	1980	1990	2000
1958:						
(Estimated total population 1955: 165,270)						
Series I	198,950	219,373	243,880	272,557	c	c
Series II	195,747	213,810	235,246	259,981	c	c
Series III	193,643	208,199	225,552	245,409	c	c
Series IV	191,517	202,541	215,790	230,834	c	c
1969:						
Series "A"	(Omitted)	(Omitted)	(Omitted)	(Omitted)	(Omitted)	(Omitted)
Series "B"	b	205,456	219,101	236,797	277,286	320,780
Series "C"	b	205,357	217,557	232,412	266,317	300,787
Series "D"	b	205,167	215,588	227,510	254,721	280,740
Series "E"	b	205,070	214,735	225,510	247,726	266,281
Series "X"[a]	b	(204,664)	c	(220,545)	(237,523)	(250,286)
1972:						
Series "A"	(Omitted)	(Omitted)	(Omitted)	(Omitted)	(Omitted)	(Omitted)
Series "B"	(Omitted)	(Omitted)	(Omitted)	(Omitted)	(Omitted)	(Omitted)
Series "C"	b	b	215,872	230,955	266,238	300,406
Series "D"	b	b	215,324	288,676	258,692	285,969
Series "E"	b	b	213,925	224,132	246,639	264,430
Series "F"	b	b	213,378	221,848	239,084	250,686

[a]"Series X" assumes "level fertility and no net immigration after 1969."

[b]Not applicable.

[c]Not available.

18

TABLE 1.7b

Increase in Population Indicated by Population Projections of the Bureau of the Census
(numbers in thousands)

Date of Projection	1955-65	1965-70	1970-75	1975-80	1970-80	1955-80	1980-90	1990-2000
1958:								
Series I	33,680	20,574	24,406	28,667	53,083	107,287	c	c
Series II	30,477	18,063	21,436	24,735	46,171	94,711	c	c
Series III	28,373	14,556	17,353	19,857	37,210	80,139	c	c
Series IV	26,247	11,024	13,249	15,044	28,293	65,664	c	c
1969:								
Series "A"	(Omitted)	(Omitted)	(Omitted)	(Omitted)	(Omitted)	b	(Omitted)	(Omitted)
Series "B"	b	b	13,645	17,696	31,341	b	40,489	43,494
Series "C"	b	b	12,200	14,855	27,055	b	33,905	34,472
Series "D"	b	b	10,421	11,922	22,343	b	27,151	26,020
Series "E"	b	b	9,665	10,775	20,440	b	22,216	18,555
Series "X"a	b	b	b	b	(15,881)	b	(16,978)	(12,763)
1972:								
Series "A"	(Omitted)	(Omitted)	(Omitted)	(Omitted)	(Omitted)	b	(Omitted)	(Omitted)
Series "B"	(Omitted)	(Omitted)	(Omitted)	(Omitted)	(Omitted)	b	(Omitted)	(Omitted)
Series "C"	b	b	b	15,083	c	b	33,907	34,168
Series "D"	b	b	b	13,352	c	b	30,016	27,272
Series "E"	b	b	b	10,207	c	b	22,507	17,791
Series "F"	b	b	b	8,470	c	b	17,231	11,602

a"Series X" assumes "level fertility and no net immigration after 1969."

bNot applicable.

cNot available.

TABLE 1.8

Numerical and Percentage Distribution of Households in the United States,
by Number of Persons, 1940, 1950, 1960, and 1970, with Numerical
and Percentage Increases During Intercensal Periods
(numbers in thousands)

Date and Census Period	Total		1-Person		2-Person		3-Person		4-Person		5-Person		6 or More	
	Number	Per-cent	Number	Per-cent	Number	Per-cent	Number	Per-cent	Number	Per-cent	Number	Per-cent	Number	Per-cent
1940	26,681	100	2,316	9	7,243	27	6,384	23	5,062	19	3,065	2	2,511	9
1950	35,934	100	3,562	10	10,518	29	8,287	23	6,655	18	3,582	10	3,333	9
1960	53,089	100	7,075	13	14,859	28	10,008	18	9,130	17	5,878	11	6,075	11
1970	63,450	100	11,146	17	18,781	29	10,909	17	9,803	15	6,198	9	6,612	11
Increases														
1940-70	36,769	136	8,830	381	11,538	159	4,525	70	4,741	93	3,133	102	4,001	153
1940-50	9,253	35	1,246	53	3,275	45	1,903	30	1,593	31	517	17	722	27
1950-60	17,155	47	3,513	100	4,341	40	1,721	20	2,475	37	2,296	64	2,742	82
1960-70	10,361	19	4,071	57	3,922	26	901	9	673	7	320	5	537	8

Sources: Computed from Census of Housing, 1940, 1950, 1960, and 1970.

The Committee gave this breakdown of the number of units needed for different purposes, as it was prepared for the Committee by Tempo, a subsidiary of General Electric:

	million units
Construction of new standard units:	
Units for new (apparently meaning additional) households	13.4
Replacement of net removals of standard units	3.0
Allowance for vacancies	1.6
Subtotal	18.0
Replacement or rehabilitation of substandard units:	
Units becoming substandard during 1968-78	2.0
Replacement of net removals	2.0
Other substandard units in the inventory in 1966	4.7
Total construction needs	26.7[21]

The estimates presented by the Department of Housing and Urban Development in April 1968 were not much different. They were as follows:

	millions
Net additional household formation	13.1
Increase in vacancies	4.4
Replace losses from inventory	7.0
Rehabilitated substandard units with subsidy	2.0
Total	26.5

In the Fourth Annual Report, the following comment was made regarding these estimates:

> Even though much progress had occurred since 1949, it was clear in the 1960's that the nation still had major housing deficiencies. The Department of Housing and Urban Development and two Presidential commissions issued reports estimating

that the housing stock still contained
between 6 and 7 million units of "substandard" housing (either dilapidated or
lacking complete plumbing). These reports also estimated the number of units
which would drop out of the stock in the
1969-78 decade because of conversion, deterioration, fires, or natural disasters.
In addition, a rapid increase in family
formation during the 1970's was projected.
Finally, there were estimates and projections of the number of low- and moderate-
income families who could not be expected
to obtain standard housing without paying
in excess of 25 percent of their income,
unless they received some kind of subsidy.[22]

The language of the Act that calls for "six million
of these [units to be constructed new or rehabilitated
should be] for low or moderate income families" has been
interpreted to mean that at least 6 of the 26 million
units to be constructed new or rehabilitated should be
made available to moderate- or low-income families by sub-
sidizing their occupancy, primarily with Federal funds, as
was indicated in the estimates presented by HUD to the
Congress. It has been so interpreted by both the Presi-
dents who have issued the Annual Report required by the
Act, summarizing progress toward the goal of 26 million
units by 1978, and the impediments and difficulties encountered in seeking to achieve a scheduled portion of
that goal.[23]

It is astonishing that the President's Committee in
the section of its report labeled "A Look at the Nation's
Housing Stock" devotes about 11 columns to a description
of what the report calls the "substandard" units (that
must be vacated and replaced), before the rest of the
stock is even mentioned.[24]

In the following pages of the Committee's Report, on
which the rest of the inventory is discussed, the Committee pointedly stated that for all families and households,
only "America's productive power" can provide relief from
intolerable housing conditions. And to be certain that
blame for the misery of enduring bad or "substandard"
housing is not laid at the doorstep of "private enterprise," the report declares that

The squalor of slum housing is not the
result of any essential defect in

America's productive power. That productive power (private enterprise sometimes joined with collaborative public policy) has shown not only that it can master space and provide unmatched abundance in the market place but also that it can produce housing.

America's existing stock of housing—more than 60 million units—is a marvel of production. When there is effective demand for it, the American housing industry can build housing with efficiency, high standards and consumer satisfaction.

Despite . . . grim statistics, the United States is a world leader in the quantity and relative quality of housing. . . .

American enterprise has built an impressive, world-leading housing inventory, and can build housing efficiently and at the highest standards, when there is effective demand for it. But American private enterprise alone cannot build housing for the poorest Americans. The rents of older houses and apartments in decent condition are regularly beyond what this low-income segment of Americans can—or should—pay.

. . . The root of the problem in housing America's poor is the gap between the price that private enterprise must receive and the price the poor can afford. In short, the basic source of the problem is not poor housing or a faulty production system. It is poverty, itself. . . .

. . . The economic gap separating millions of deprived families from adequate housing can only be bridged by government subsidies. Such subsidies create an effective and real market demand to which private enterprise has proved it will respond with volume production, providing there is opportunity for earning a reasonable profit.[25]

The implication in this eulogy of the construction industry is that once a house has received the ministrations of this "efficient" and progressive "industry," it

can no longer be considered an actual or potential part
of the supply of units available to those who seek "adequate" housing; only first-hand new housing can be considered "adequate." If seekers of housing for occupancy
are unable to pay "the price that private enterprise must
receive [for the new house]," the public must subsidize
the home seeker by whatever amount is necessary to enable
him to meet that price.

Then the so-called "private industry" will be assured
of the disposition of its product at a price that will
yield for it what it considers to be a "reasonable profit"
and will again perform its characteristic "marvel of production." And it's only by this kind of process in which
"private enterprise [is] sometimes joined with collaborative public policy" that the poor can ever be provided
with "adequate" housing! (Notwithstanding the praise of
the existing inventory, every unit that has once been
occupied is no longer a "new" product of the building industry.)

NOTES

1. Section 1601, Public Law 90-488, approved August
1, 1968.

2. "Housing Needs--A Preliminary Estimate," National
Housing Bulletin (November 1944) (Washington, D.C.: National Housing Agency), p. 6.

3. Ibid., p. 6.

4. Majority Report of the Joint Congressional Committee on Housing, March 15, 1948.

5. HHFA, Annual Report, 1958.

6. Report of Subcommittee on Housing (under Senate
Resolution 221) to the Committee on Banking and Currency,
86th Congress, 2nd Session, April 15, 1960, p. 1.

7. Ibid., p. 14.

8. Ibid., p. 19.

9. Ibid., pp. 22, 23.

10. Ibid., p. 25.

11. Ibid., p. 74.

12. Ibid., p. 70.

13. Ibid., p. 72.

14. HHFA Annual Report, 1960, p. 17.

15. Ibid., p. 8.

16. Ibid. Presumably it is not to be inferred that
foreclosures are nothing to worry about until they reach
the level attained in the delirious 1930s; but that is
close to what this comment suggests.

17. *HHFA Annual Report*, 1960, p. 16.
18. Ibid., p. 14.
19. U.S. Bureau of the Census, *Current Population of the United States and Components of Change: 1972* (with annual data from 1930), Series P-25, No. 499, May 1973.
20. "A Decent Home," The Report of the President's Committee on Urban Housing (Washington, D.C.: Government Printing Office, 1969), p. 1.
21. Ibid., p. 40.
22. *Fourth Annual Report on National Housing Goals* (Washington, D.C.: Government Printing Office, 1972), p. 25.
23. See the First, Second, Third, and Fourth *Annual Reports on National Housing Goals, Messages from the President of The United States* transmitting the *Report on National Housing Goals, Pursuant to the Provisions of the Housing and Urban Development Act of 1968* (Washington, D.C.: Government Printing Office, 1969, 1970, 1971, and 1972).
24. President's Committee on Urban Housing, *Report*, pp. 43, 44, and 45.
25. Ibid., pp. 45, 46, and 47.

2

STANDING STOCK AS
AN "ADEQUATE HOUSING"
RESOURCE

The previous chapter has outlined the principal steps by which the average annual volume of 2 million new and 600,000 rehabilitated units for the decade following the election year of 1968 was established. Those are the overt reasons why the President's Committee on Urban Housing, the President's Commission on Urban Problems, and the officers of the Federal governmental agencies recommended this volume of building, and why the Congress declared these numbers sacrosanct, not to be "touched" by hoi polloi, nor even by the high priests of the Executive Branch, regardless of the political party to which they presumably give dutiful obeisance.

The sacrosanct number, 20 million new units to be built during a ten-year span, is (to repeat) about a third more than the 15 million units built during the fantastic 1950s, and about two-thirds as many as were built during the decades of both the 1940s and the 1950s. But these were the decades during which the great migrations from farms and villages to the big metropolitan areas and from the snows and ice of the North and East to the sunshine and year-round warmth of Florida, California, and other newly recognized resort sections of the country were at their peak; when the millions of soldiers, sailors, and airmen who had served in World War II were being discharged and were entering civilian careers and settling their families. Upon what base did the projection of a program of this magnitude rest in 1968?

It must be remembered that the two objectives, either pronounced or implied, in all these projections of residential construction volume were to provide a "decent home in a suitable environment for every American family," and to stabilize the residential construction industry. To accomplish the first of these objectives, all the committees' reports and the reports of officials of the Executive Branch placed almost exclusive emphasis upon the construction of new units to be made available to the lower-middle- and low-income families or households; and to attain the objective of stabilization of the industry, emphasis was almost exclusively on inducement of a volume of new construction that was set in 1943 at the level of 1.3 million units a year and finally reached by 1968 the unprecedented level of 2 million units a year.

These objectives are unchallengeable; but it is difficult to follow the reasoning that emphasized their attainment by inducing the construction of new units. To insist upon building the most expensive and most durable product in our economy for even all families, not to mention households,[1] when new construction adds only 3 percent to the whole inventory in a year, is to ignore the principal source of housing facilities.

During the whole decade of the 1960s only a little more than 14 million units were started, while at the beginning of the decade, according to the Bureau of the Census, there were not less than 10 million single-family units valued by their owner-occupants at $10,000 or less, 14 million valued at less than $12,500, and 18 million units valued at less than $15,000.

But of the 3.9 million <u>new</u> units sold from 1963 through 1970, on which sales price was reported, only 255,000 were sold for less than $12,500, and only 596,000 for less than $15,000 (see Table 2.1).

According to the Census of Housing, 1970, there were more than 32 million owner-occupied and "vacant for sale" units, 2 million of which their owners reported to be worth less than $5,000; more than 7 million valued at less than $10,000; and 13.6 million at less than $15,000 (see Table 2.1).

It is estimated that the rate of turnover of owner-occupancy houses is between 10 and 12 percent a year and that the average term of ownership and occupancy is eight or ten years. At this rate of turnover, on the average, between 3.2 and 4 million of these units must have been bought and sold <u>annually</u> between 1960 and 1970. And some 700,000 of these units probably cost their purchasers less than $10,000; and between 1,350,000 and 1,080,000 of them less than $15,000.

But during the whole period of 1963 to 1970 less than 4 million <u>new</u> houses were sold, and only 596,000 of

27

TABLE 2.1

Numerical and Percentage Distribution in 1960 and 1970 of Owner-Occupied and
"Vacant for Sale" Housing Units by Value Classes and of Single-Family
Units Sold, 1963-70, by Price Classes

Value and Price Classes	Owner-Occupied, 1960[a]		Owner-Occupied, 1970[b]		New Homes Sold, 1963-70	
	Number[c]	Percent	Number[d]	Percent[e]	Number[f]	Percent
Total	26	100	32	100	3,879	100
Less than $5,000	3	12	2	6	NA	NA
Less than $10,000	10	26	7	22	NA	NA
Less than $12,500	14	39	10	32	255	7
Less than $15,000	18	53	14	42	596	15
Less than $20,000	23	62	20	62	1,619	44
$20,000 or more	3	38	12	38	2,177	56

[a]Owner-occupied only, 1960.
[b]Owner-occupied and vacant for sale, 1970.
[c]Rounded to millions.
[d]The number owner-occupied only.
[e]Percentage owner-occupied only.
[f]Rounded to thousands.

Sources: U.S. Bureau of the Census, Census of Housing, 1960, vol. 1, "States and Small Areas"; Part 1, United States Summary (Washington, D.C.: Government Printing Office, 1963), p. 34; "General Housing Characteristics," 1970, Final Report, p. 55, Table 17.

these cost their purchasers less than $15,000. If these
calculations are within an acceptable margin of error, the
existing inventory provided as many houses for sale at
less than $15,000 in one year as the building industry
provided in all price ranges in five years (see Table 2.1).

After all, the market has not been entirely neglectful
of households in the lower-middle- or even the low-income
groups.

In 1970, more than 50 percent of the households in
the United States whose incomes were under $3,000 owned
the homes they occupied; and if one should assume that
households with incomes between $7,500 and $10,000 represent the lower-middle-income group, he would find that the
market has functioned so as to enable more than 68 percent
of these to become home owners (see Table 2.2).

Further the Bureau of the Census reports that more
than two-thirds of the households that bought homes from
1963 to 1969 bought previously occupied, not new, homes
(see Table 2.3). About 10 percent of the purchasers of
new homes in 1969 reported their incomes were less than
$5,000; 35 percent, less than $10,000. But only 66,000 of
the former income group had been served by the new house
market; while 327,000--about five times as many--must have
found an acceptable home among the previously occupied
homes whose owners wanted to sell (see Table 2.2).

Surely, meeting the needs of the low- and lower-
middle-income groups does not depend solely upon the productive capacity of the residential building industry,
"joined with collaborative public policy," that provides
subsidies sufficient to "bridge the gap between . . . the
price the poor can afford" and "the price that private
enterprise [that is, private builders] must receive [in]
. . . earning a reasonable profit."

Similarly, the existing stock serves a large portion
of the "low- and lower-middle-income" group that rent
their homes. At the time of the Census of Housing, 1970,
there were 23.9 million housing units that were occupied
by renters or "vacant, available for rent." Obviously,
these served all income groups. For these rented units
are reported to have commanded rents that varied from
"less than $30" to "$200 or more" a month. Nearly 10 percent of the units were reported to rent for $40 a month
or less; 20 percent for $60 a month or less; and more than
half under $100 a month.

In contrast, of 254,000 units in apartment houses
built and rented during the year 1970, less than 3 percent
rented for less than $125 a month, only 14 percent for

TABLE 2.2

Percentage Distribution of Home Owners in 1970, by Income Classes and Numerical and Percentage Distribution of Purchasers of New and Previously Occupied Homes During 1969, by Income Classes
(numbers in thousands)

| Income Classes | Percent Homeowners 1970 | Age of Home Purchased | | | | | |
| | | Total | | Previously Occupied | | New Homes | |
		Number	Percent	Number	Percent	Number	Percent
Total	64.0	2,703	100	1,979	100	724	100
Under $3,000	50.3	170	6.2	132	6.6	38	5.2
$3,000 to $4,999	55.6	223	8.2	195	9.8	28	3.8
Under $5,000	NA	393	14.5	327	16.5	66	9.1
$5,000 to $7,499	55.5	520	19.2	456	23.0	64	8.8
$7,500 to $9,999	68.2	479	17.7	353	17.8	126	17.4
Under $10,000	NA	1,392	51.4	1,136	57.4	256	35.2
$10,000 to $14,999	77.2	688	25.4	470	24.2	209	28.8
$15,000 and more	84.5	500	18.4	299	15.1	201	27.2
Not reported		124	4.5	66	3.3	58	8.0

Source: U.S. Bureau of the Census, Current Population Reports, "Consumer Buying Indicators," Series P-65, No. 33, June 12, 1970.

TABLE 2.3

Numerical and Percentage Distribution of Housing Units Rented
and for Rent and of Units in Apartment Houses Built and
Rented in 1970, by Monthly Rent

Gross Rent Classes	Renter Occupied and Available		Built and Rented, 1970	
	Number[a]	Percent	Number	Percent
Total	23,999	100	253,834	100
Under $30	999[b]	4.4[b]	NA	NA
Under $40	2,068	8.6	NA	NA
Under $60	5,262	22.4	NA	NA
Under $80	9,665	40.4	NA	NA
Under $100	13,163	55.0	NA	NA
Less than $125	NA	NA	7,265	2.8
Under $150	19,027	79.5	34,598	13.6
$150 or more	3,273[b]	14.6[b]	219,236	86.3
Under $200	21,477	89.8	NA	NA
$200 or more	1,104	4.6	101,070	39.8
No cash	1,094[b]	4.0	NA	NA

[a]The numbers in this column are rounded to thousands.
[b]This is the number renter-occupied and the percentage of all renter-occupied, and not of total.

Sources: U.S. Bureau of the Census, Census of Housing, 1970; "General Housing Characteristics," Final Report, p. 28; ibid., with Department of Housing and Urban Development, Housing Reports, "Market Absorption of Apartments," H-130, August 10, 1970, February 11, 1971, and May 20, 1971.

TABLE 2.4

Number of Homes Bought for Owner Occupancy by Years, with
Percentage Consisting of Previously Occupied Units
(numbers in thousands)

Year	Total	New	Previously Occupied	Percentage of Total Previously Occupied
Total	17,474	5,907	11,567	66.1
1963	1,944	732	1,212	62.3
1964	1,755	590	1,165	66.3
1965	2,155	741	1,414	65.6
1966	2,033	711	1,322	65.0
1967	2,301	663	1,638	71.1
1968	2,773	969	1,804	65.0
1969	3,203	1,085	2,118	66.1

Source: U.S. Bureau of the Census, Current Population Reports, "Consumer Buying Indicators," Series P-65, No. 33, October 16, 1970, p. 18.

less than $150; and 40 percent for $200 a month or more.
In brief, rents in these new units began at a figure that
was higher than rents charged for 60 percent of the standing stock (see Table 2.3). One of the major contributors
to this wide disparity between rents in the standing stock
and those charged for units in newly built structures is
that nearly all the units for rent new are in structures
containing more than one unit; that is, in multifamily
structures. Rents in the larger of these structures,
apartment houses, must be high enough to cover the costs
of operation, which in the larger structures not uncommonly
amount to as much as 40 percent of the total rent charged.
But nearly 39 percent of renter-occupied units in the
whole country were reported in 1970 to be in single-family
structures; 27 percent of the rented units in Standard
Metropolitan Statistical Areas; and even in the Central
Cities of SMSAs, one in five renting households live in
single-family structures.[2]

The extent to which this portion of renting households
is entirely neglected by the "efficient," "private-
enterprise" "building industry" is suggested by the fact
that of all new one-family houses started from 1963 to
1970 for which the "purpose of construction" was reported
(7 million), only less than 2 percent (123,000) were reported to have been built to rent.[3]

Now, if, as reported in the 1970 Census of Housing,
40 percent (9.7 million) of the renting households acquired their housing units during the 15 months preceding
the date of the Census, and more than 1.6 million units
were vacant and available for rent on that date, then better than half the existing rented and for rental units
became available for occupancy at some time during these
15 months. And it is reasonable to suppose that these
were evenly distributed in the rent ranges. If these
assumptions be true, about three times the number of units
produced for rent, all of which were rented in the upper
rental brackets, became available for occupancy during the
year 1963, the year when the largest number of rental
units ever produced came on the market (see Table 2.3).[4]

1. Although the Secretary of Housing and Urban Development and the Administrator of the HHFA in their Annual Reports and the President's Committee on Urban Housing in its Report frequently used the terms "family" and "household" as though they were interchangeable, it is evident from the numbers cited that in most cases it was household that was intended. Keeping these terms separate is important for the following reasons, among others: (1) in 1970, 11,637,000 households, 18 percent of the total, were not families; (2) the mean number of persons per family in 1970 was 3.62; that of other households was 1.21; (3) less than 60 percent of the increase in households from 1960 to 1970 was accounted for by the increase in families; (4) the household, which may consist of one person living alone or with one or more persons unrelated by blood, marriage, or adoption, is obviously a much less stable social unit than the family; hence that portion of the demand for housing units that is attributable to households is much more volatile than that which comes from families. See U.S. Bureau of the Census, Current Population Reports, "Household and Family Characteristics," March 1971 (Washington, D.C.: Government Printing Office, 1972) (Tables V and VII).

2. U.S. Bureau of the Census, Census of Housing, 1970, "General Housing Characteristics," Final Report, HC(1)-A, U.S. Summary (Washington, D.C.: Government Printing Office), pp. 16, 53.

3. U.S. Bureau of the Census, Construction Reports, Series C-25, "Characteristics of New One-Family Homes, 1970" (Washington, D.C.: U.S. Department of Commerce, 1971), p. 7.

4. These estimates are based on the Census of Housing, 1970. In "Detailed Housing Characteristics," Final Report, HC(1)-B1, United States Summary, p. 234, it is reported that 21.5 percent of all units occupied at the date of the census had been moved into in "1969 and 1970" (that is, before the census was taken as of April 1). Since the total number occupied at that date was given as 63,455,192, about 13,450,331 units had been moved into during the 15-month period January 1, 1969, to April 1, 1970. If it is assumed that these moves were evenly distributed over the 15 months, then about 900,000 were made monthly or at the rate of 10.8 million a year. Table 3, page 16, "General Characteristics," U.S. Summary HC(1)-A1, gives the total number of owner-occupied units at the time of the census as 39,885,000; renter-occupied at 23,565,000; total

63,450,000. If the average term of owner-occupancy is assumed to be ten years, 3,988,000 of the 13,450,000 "move-
ins" would be accounted for. The remaining 9.4 units
would have been moved into by renters. And 9.4 million is
just 40 percent of the total number of rental units occupied. An additional 1,583,000 units were specified "vacant for rent." If these are added to the 9.4 million
units presumed to have been occupied during the year, the
total number that were or became vacant during the year
reached 11 million--nearly half of the total number occupied or available for occupancy by renters.

**THE ROLE OF "USED" AND
NEW HOUSING IN SERVING
LOW- AND MIDDLE-
INCOME HOUSEHOLDS**

There is another way in which the markets for previously occupied houses and those for new houses serve in
combination the needs of the low- and lower-middle-income
households: when a new house is bought and occupied by
the occupiers of an existing unit, the unit they vacate
comes on the market for occupancy by another household;
and the unit this household vacates becomes available to
another, and so on, to the end of the chain of events that
begins with the occupancy of a new unit. Little has been
known about the character of the chain of events initiated
by the original purchase of the new house; but a pioneer-
ing study made recently at the University of Michigan has
thrown some light upon it.[1]

The study was made of the chain reaction of events
that was set in motion by the purchase and occupancy of a
sample of 1,133 newly occupied homes--a sample that was
chosen to represent "roughly . . . all standard metropolitan statistical areas in the U.S. with a population of
200,000 or more in the central city." The study "stresses
the question of whether the housing market operates in
such a way that new construction indirectly benefits the
poor in general. . . ?" It also "exploits the material
collected . . . to contribute to an understanding of the
demand for new housing."[2]

The principal conclusions reached by the study may
be summarized as follows:

1. For every 1,000 new homes built
and occupied, approximately 3,500 households
moved into what was for them a different
home; in some cases as many as nineteen

households moved into quarters vacated as
the result of the first transaction.

2. Six percent of the purchasers of
new homes were households with incomes less
than $3,000; 7 percent of the movers in the
first chain reaction were in this income
group; 14 percent of those in the second;
14 percent of those in the third; 16 percent
of those in the next rank; 13 percent of all
the movers in the entire chain reaction were
in this income group. To quote the study
directly: "We can conclude that the poor
are indirectly affected by the construction
of new housing even if they do not occupy
the new dwellings."

3. Sixty-six percent of the movers
classified by the study as "poor" reported
that they liked the home they moved to
"better" and 24 percent "about the same" as
the one from which they moved.

It seems strange that this important source of housing facilities available to the low- and lower-middle-
income households could have been given so little attention by the officials of HHFA and HUD, by the committees
of the Congress, and by most of the official studies and
reports that have been made on housing since the days of
the President's Conference of Home Building and Home
Ownership held in Washington in 1931.*

---

*The Conference was called by President Hoover and
was organized and presided over by two members of his
Cabinet, Robert P. Lamont and Ray Lyman Wilbur, Secre-
taries of Commerce and of the Interior. The Co-Chairmen
appointed 25 fact-finding committees and six correlating
committees. Altogether, there were 558 members of these
committees, and "more than 3,700 persons registered as
members of the Conference," according to the final report.
The reports of the fact-finding committees, and of the
discussions at the Conference were published in 11 volumes, copyrighted 1933 by the President's Conference on
Home Building and Home Ownership. The costs of the Conference were defrayed, it was commonly said, from surplus
funds left at the disposal of the President when he was
serving as relief administrator in Belgium after World
War I.

It was this conference that focused the public attention and the interest of both the legislative and the executive branches of the Federal government on the subject. At that time, and during the succeeding six years, while five or more major legislative enactments were being discussed and enacted in Washington, unemployment in the building trades was pervasive. Residential construction had shrunk to about one-tenth of the volume it reached at the peak of 1926, and vacancies were much higher in most urban communities than ever before in the memory of most observers of urban real estate and housing markets.

LEGISLATION PROMOTING NEW HOUSING

One of the principal purposes of the President's Conference and of all of this legislation of the 1930s was to revive the comatose residential construction industry, diminish unemployment of building tradesmen, and revive the building materials production and distribution industries. These purposes were perpetuated and strengthened by the passage of the Full Employment Act of 1946, and have dominated housing legislation and its administration ever since. No--or at most, very little--attention has been given and very little comment made on the effects on legislative and administrative action that full employment in these trades and activities of post-World War II years should have had. Almost the entire drive of both the legislative and the executive branches of the Federal government has been concentrated on increasing the volume of residential construction, even when vacancies and mortgage delinquencies and foreclosures were rising.

The Federal actions seem to have been intended to stabilize the residential construction industry at a level that has risen continuously since the first estimate of the number of new units needed to "provide for . . . making up past deficiencies" was published in 1944. Since 1964 (or thereabout) the urgent appeal has been to increase the contribution of this segment of the national economy to the gross national product. And when the number of units produced by the industry has dropped below its highest previous peak, the housing authorities of the Federal government have joined with leaders of the home building industry and of labor unions in crying out "housing crisis."[3]

Obviously, there is no longer the kind of general or nation-wide housing crisis that confronted the nation at the end of World War II.[4]

As one well-informed observer remarked recently in
private conversation, "There is only a crisis in some
parts of some of our larger metropolitan complexes."

But the official line seems to be still to shout loud
cries of "crisis."

To these local limited crises, it may not be entirely
amiss to suggest that some of the actions or policies of
the government itself may be contributing: insistence
upon building new homes for the occupancy of lower-middle-
and lower-income families may be accelerating the rate at
which much of the existing stock in some parts of some of
our metropolitan areas is deteriorating--even to the point
of abandonment by private owners. Many of these structures could have been, and still could be, saved for occupancy under much better conditions than they present now
at costs that would not have been even a major part of
what the new units that have been built by public housing
authorities in many communities have cost.

And some of these newly built and costly structures
have already come to the point of abandonment, after a
life span of only two or three decades.[5]

NEW HOMES ARE FOR INCREMENTAL DEMAND

The thinking and actions of Federal officials seem to
have been based upon the assumption that houses, like food
or clothing (or automobiles), are commodities that are
quickly consumed and therefore must be replaced after a
brief period of use. If this were so, a boom decade would
have produced a supply that, in the hands of consumers,
would have to be replaced within, say, a decade or so,
plus the additional units needed to provide for increases
of households.

But the well-built and well-cared-for housing unit
has a life of nearer a hundred than ten years. Conse-
quently, the major portion of new construction is needed
for increase in consuming units, not for replacement of
the existing stock.

And urban housing consuming units do not increase at
a constant rate, especially after the whole society has
been disturbed and its behavior patterns disrupted by a
four- or five-year total war or a prolonged 1930s depression. Such a national episode greatly accelerates or de-
presses the rate of growth of households and the production of heads of future households. The question is not
whether it is desirable to stabilize urban residential

construction; it is the much more complicated one of how to stabilize the production of the most durable economic goods in the nation, when the major force that determines the volume of "need" fluctuates from decade to decade by a large increment or decrement;[6] when one-fifth of the consuming units move every year; and when the items in the inventory are fixed in location. It is the much more difficult problem of trying to determine the level of production that will meet the imminent need for shelter of households that are not currently in existence and that may come and go on short notice, while the provision for their needs stays fixed in location for a century or more --and still not waste resources by providing these facilities at locations and at such times that their provision is not synchronized with the preferences and needs of the consuming units.

It is especially difficult to project the volume of new construction that will be needed in the years following a decade or more of rapid increase in the number of households that have appeared in a local market area.* Extrapolation of the current rate of increase may lead to overbuilding; reduction in the annual volume of production may lead to stringent housing shortage if the increase in the number of households continues at the current rate (and certainly to unemployment and a reduction in the total community income). The demand or need for additional units--that is, incremental demand--may increase or decrease by as much as 100 percent in a single year. When it decreases, continuation of the current rate of construction may lead to a wasteful overexpansion of the inventory and of the resources required to create the excess--all because the items, once in the inventory, stay there--exactly where they are built--for three or four generations, but each generation lives its own lives where it pleases.

The increase of population in the age groups of which the heads of households are members has been, since the

---

*It may be worth while to notice here that the increase in the number of nonfarm households that occurred during the 1960s was only one million more than in the 1950s; while the increase during the 1950s was two million more than in the 1940s. The rate of increase declined during the 1960s from 31 percent realized during the 1950s, to 25 percent during the 1960s--a decline of 20 percent.

beginning of the present century, very unstable, and yet
the product of the residential building industry that is
intended to serve them survives not only their term of
occupancy, but also that of their children's children,
"even unto the third and fourth generation."

In estimating the number of units that would be needed
to accommodate the additional households that would be
formed between 1968 and 1978, the President's Committee on
Urban Housing and the Congress, in following the recommendations of this Committee and of the officials of HUD, set
down the number at 13.4 million units. This was the same
number as the Bureau of the Census had set down in its
1958 Series I projection as the largest probable number to
be established between the years 1970 and 1980. The
smallest number, presented in the Series "D," was 10.6
million.

But the Bureau had made another group of projections
in 1965, raising the numbers suggested in each of the two
series published in that year: from 13.0 million as the
largest, to 14 million; and the smallest likely number
from 10.6 million to 12.3. These projections were revised again in 1972, and the largest increase for the
period 1975 to 1980 was estimated at 7.2 million, and the
smaller at 6.6 million. Thus the two sets of projections
varied little in the average number per annum that might
be realized during the decade of the 1970s. The final
numbers in the 1972 projections fell between an average
of 1.4 and 1.3 million a year (see Table 3.1).

If it is assumed that a new unit must be provided for
every increase of one in nonfarm households, then the 13
million units proposed by the President's Committee on
Urban Housing is reasonable. But it must be remembered
that, so far as the statistics we have can be relied upon,
the nonfarm inventory has increased by a larger number
than have nonfarm households in every decade since 1920,
except for the decade of the 1960s, when starts exceeded
the increase in the number in the inventory by some 102
million (see Table 3.2).[7] And in the 1950s, the increase
in the inventory was only about 76,000 more than starts.
During the whole period 1920 to 1970 total starts reported
amounted to 44.4 million units, while the increase in the
nonfarm inventory numbered 48.2 million (see Tables 1.1
and 1.3).

Starts thus amounted to about 96 percent of the increase in the inventory. If it is assumed that a similar
ratio will prevail in the 1920s, then the number of new
units needed will fall between 12.6 and 11.8 million, or
an average of 1,260,000 and 1,180,000 a year.

40

TABLE 3.1

U.S. Bureau of the Census Projections of Number of Households
in the United States at Selected Dates
(numbers in thousands)

Date of Projections	Future Date				
	1960	1965	1970	1975	1980
1956[a]					
Series I	51,835	56,143	61,378	67,378	--
Series II	51,573	55,579	60,762	66,480	--
Series III	51,000	54,474	58,988	64,312	--
Series IV	50,499	53,345	57,110	61,584	--
1958[b]					
Series A	52,425	57,517	62,933	69,318	76,006
Series B	51,877	56,076	61,094	67,003	73,085
Series C	51,614	55,311	59,689	64,906	70,544
Series D	51,350	54,565	58,814	63,900	69,382
1962[c]					
Series A	--	58,637	63,865	70,036	76,494
Series B	--	57,195	62,023	67,730	73,601
1965[d]					
Series 1	--	--	63,300	70,001	77,308
Series 2	--	--	62,425	68,229	74,728
1972[e]					
Series 1	--	--	--	70,078	77,296
Series 2	--	--	--	69,408	76,063

	Projected Increase over Projection Period			
	1960-70	1970-80	1975-80	Average per Annum
1958				
Series A	9,543	13,073	6,688	1,337
Series B	9,217	11,991	6,082	1,216
Series C	8,075	10,855	5,638	1,107
Series D	7,464	10,568	5,485	1,097
1965				
Series 1	--	14,008	7,307	1,461
Series 2	--	12,303	6,499	1,292
1972				
Series 1	--		7,218	1,443
Series 2	--		6,665	1,331

Sources:
[a]Current Population Reports, "Population Characteristics,"
Series P-20, No. 69, August 31, 1956, p. 1.
[b]Current Population Reports, "Population Characteristics,"
Series P-20, No. 90, December 29, 1958, p. 1.
[c]Statistical Abstract, 1965, p. 36.
[d]Statistical Abstract, 1970, p. 36.
[e]Current Population Reports, "Population Estimates and Projections," Demographic Projections for United States, Series P-25,
No. 476, February 1972, p. 24.

TABLE 3.2

Increases in Population from 1970 to 1980 (or 1975 to 1980) Suggested by the Projections of the U.S. Bureau of the Census Made in 1960, 1969, and 1972, with the Ratio of These Projected Increases to the Number of New Dwelling Units Proposed to be Constructed in Accordance with the Provisions of the Act of 1968

	Population Projections of 1960			Population Projections of 1969			Population Projections of 1972		
	Number	Ratio to Number of New Units	New Units per 100 Population Increase	Number	Ratio to Number of New Units	Number of New Units per 100 Population Increase	Number	Ratio to Number of New Units	Number of New Units per 100 Population Increase
Series I ("A")	53,083	2.65	37.6	Omitted	--	--	Omitted	Omitted	--
Series II ("B")	46,161	2.30	43.3	31,341	1.56	63.8	Omitted	Omitted	--
Series III ("C")	37,210	1.86	53.7	27,055	1.35	72.9	15,083	1.51	66.2
Series IV ("D")	28,293	1.41	70.6	22,343	1.11	89.5	13,152	1.31	76.0
Series "E"	--	--	--	20,440	1.01	97.8	10,207	1.03	97.9
Series "F"*	--	--	--	--	--	--	8,470	0.84	118.0

*Series "F" numbers are for the years 1975 to 1980.

Sources: Current Population Reports, Population Estimates and Projections, "Demographic Projections for the United States," Series P-25, No. 476, February, 1972, p. 24; Current Population Reports, Population Estimates and Projections, "Projections of the population of the United States, by Age and Sex, 1972 to 2020"; Series P-25, No. 493, December, 1972; Statistical Abstract, 1965, p. 6.

If one places the ratio at 100 percent, the number of
new units needed would fall between 14.0 and 13.9 million
--or an average of 1,440,000 and 1,350,000 a year (see
Tables 1.5 and 3.1).

There is one other calculation that is helpful in
making this kind of projection: by dividing the projected
population increase suggested by each of the Bureau of the
Census' Series by the number of households suggested in
each of its series, one can see what the average or mean
number of persons per household would be in 1980.

The results of such a calculation indicate that if
the largest projected increase in population (Series "B")
should be realized, and the smallest number of households
should be formed (Series 2), in 1980, the average household would consist of about 3.11 persons. If the reverse
situation should come about, and total population should
only reach 255.6 million, living in 77,296 households, the
average would be only 2.91 persons. But it must be noticed
that all persons do not live in households. Hence, the
average number of persons per household would be slightly
smaller than is indicated here.

Another very suggestive calculation seems worthwhile:
if the numbers suggested in Series "B" projection made in
1969 (a series that was omitted from the 1972 projection),
and the quota of 20 million units were built during the
decade, we should have built a new unit for every increase
of 1.56 persons in the population. If the population increased by only 20,440,000 as suggested by Series "E," we
should have built a new unit for every increase of 1.01
persons; and if Series "F," which was added in the 1972
projection, should turn out to be the most accurate of
all the projections made up to and including 1972, we
should have built a new unit for every increase of 0.84
persons, or 118 new units for every increase of 100 in
the population (see Table 3.2).

Taking all these calculations into consideration, it
seems that an allowance of 13 million as the largest and
10 or 11 million as the smallest number of new units
likely to be needed to meet the increment in demand caused
by increase in population would be more realistic than the
single figure of 13.4 million.

One source of increase in nonfarm population during
the 1950s was migration from the farms. During this
decade, this number has been estimated at 10.5 million--
more than a million a year. And during the first seven
years of the 1960s, it is estimated to have been 6.6 million. But these 6.6 million farm-to-city migrants were
drawn from a total farm population in 1960 of 15.6 million,

TABLE 3.3

Estimated U.S. Farm Population, 1950 to 1972, with
Annual Numerical Decrease (or Increase)
for Selected Terms of Years
(numbers in thousands)

	Population			Annual Migration
Year	Total	Decrease	Year	Number of Emigrants
1950	23,048	--	1950	1,537
1951	21,890	1,158	1951	1,531
1952	21,748	142	1952	483
1953	19,874	1,874	1953	2,201
1954	19,019	855	1954	1,151
1955	19,078	+59	1955	210
1956	18,712	366	1956	627
1957	17,656	1,056	1957	1,295
1958	17,128	528	1958	748
1959	16,592	536	1959	740
1960	15,635	957	1960	1,142
1961	14,803	832	1961	1,000
1962	14,313	490	1962	646
1963	13,367	946	1963	1,086
1964	12,954	413	1964	533
1965	12,363	591	1965	703
1966	11,595	768	1966	858
1967	10,875	720	1967	793
1968	10,454	421	1968	481
1969	10,307	147	1969	198
1970	9,712	595	1970	642
1971	9,425	287	1971	330
1972	9,610	+185	1972	+157

Sources: Statistical Abstract, 1971, p. 572; Statistical Abstract, 1973, p. 584.

which had fallen by 1967 to 10.9 million. This 1967 pool was no longer large enough to supply cityward migrants at an average rate of a million a year--at least, not for many years. It should have been obvious in 1967 that the annual increase of nonfarm population from this source was almost certain to shrink during the coming decade (see Table 3.3). During the period 1950 through 1957, 9,035,000 persons migrated from farms; during the corresponding years of the 1960s, this number dropped to 6.6 million, about 24 percent. This was a sufficient change in direction of the series to raise serious questions about the continuation of this source of growth in the population of urban communities before the 26 million quota was recommended to the Congress.

NOTES

1. The first study of the sort was made by Frank Kristof in the summer of 1963. See his "Federal Housing Policies: Subsidized Production, Filtration and Objectives: Part II," Land Economics 49 (May 1973) 2, which also gives a good summary of the study made at the University of Michigan.

2. John B. Lansing, Charles Wade Clifton, and James N. Morgan, "New Homes and Poor People," Survey Research Center, Institute for Social Research, University of Michigan (1969), especially pp. iv, 13, 23, 37, 39, 41, and 65-69. The date of purchase of the new homes studied is not given; interviews with purchasers and "movers" in the chain were conducted in 1966 and 1967.

3. This fever evidently infected the Republican administration when it assumed office in January 1969. In its first Annual Report, the Department of Housing and Urban Development asserted that

> The year 1969 was a crisis time in housing.
> . . . Secretary George Romney announced
> operation "Breakthrough" . . . to help ease
> the housing crisis . . . [and] to break
> through the major obstacles to volume pro-
> duction, marketing and delivery of housing
> for all income levels. The Secretary of
> Housing and Urban Development administers a
> wide range of programs to . . . stimulate
> and assist production of sufficient housing
> of good quality for all citizens at every
> income level. . . . He directs Federal

45

> efforts to enlist private home-building and
> mortgage-lending institutions in efforts to
> alleviate the housing shortage.

U.S. Department of Housing and Urban Development, <u>Annual
Report, 1969</u> (Washington, D.C.: Government Printing Office), p. 9.

4. As early as 1952, the HHFA in its <u>Annual Report</u>
for that year (p. 3) stated that "Now the post-war backlog
has largely been met [sic!]."

5. While two robins still do not make a spring, one
cannot ignore the implications of the following item that
appeared in one of the official publications of the Department of Housing and Urban Development: "The St. Louis
Housing Authority is soliciting bids for the demolition of
two Pruitt-Igoe buildings. HUD has approved the demolition
. . . which would serve several purposes: thin the density
of the project; provide accurate cost figures for demolition; and open up additional space within the project for
recreational use." HUD <u>Newsletter</u> 2 (December 27, 1971)
48:4. Pruitt-Igoe was built in the early 1950s. A similar
fate appears to be in store for the largest project in
Newark, N.J.

In the continued pressure for more work for building tradesmen and housing builders, public authorities seem
to have forgotten or at least ignored the question of how
their endeavors and their programs may have impinged upon
the decaying portions of the inner cities. There appears
to be no solid basis of facts and serious studies upon
which administrative and executive decisions such as those
represented by the recently issued regulations of HUD setting forth the priorities for allocation of funds to the
local government units applying for them can be formulated.

6. See, for example, Arthur F. Burns, "Long Cycles
in Residential Construction," in <u>Economic Essays in Honor
of Wesley Clair Mitchell</u> (New York: Columbia University
Press, 1935), p. 63.

7. There is some confusion over the method of counting the number of "new or rehabilitated units" that the
Congress has decreed as its mandate. Generally, it has
been assumed that the number of starts as reported by the
Bureau of the Census constitutes the goal. But the Nixon
administration added the number of mobile homes shipped
from factory to the number of starts; and the number of
reported starts is quite different from the number reported
completed within a given period. Cf. also Edward F.
Henshaw, "The Demand for Housing in the Mid-1970's," <u>Land
Economics</u> 47 (August 1973) 3:249.

46

4

ELIMINATION OF "SUBSTANDARD" HOUSING UNITS

The stubborn persistence of units of the standing stock brings to housing markets another intractable and unique feature: very few of the units are ever "consumed" in the sense that they are "used up." They become obsolete; they deteriorate and go "out of style"; they come to represent a standard of living with respect to housing that is condemned by many as a menace to the health, safety, and welfare of their occupants--but they seldom are worn out. Those that are actually torn down are destroyed usually to make way for other kinds of construction, such as highways, public buildings, or other types of privately owned buildings.

But, since they are so durable, many housing structures survive these hazards and persist through generations of technological, public health, safety, and welfare advances.

As a result, in every industrial society, there stand many residential structures that provide some privacy and some protection from inclement weather and obtrusive crime, but not many of those other services that have come to be regarded by the majority of public opinion as essential.

These units are called "substandard." And when officials or others make projections of the number of new units that they believe should be constructed over a future period, a number is always inserted for replacing these, or a major portion of these that the projectors consider to be, or are about to become, "substandard."

Now let it be understood clearly that no one with a live conscience would desire to keep any household in a unit that does constitute a menace to its occupants' and its neighbors' health, safety, and welfare. This is universally agreed. But since the first days of housing census-taking, during the 1930s, no way of determining how many such units there are in any community of size has been discovered. Hence, there can be no consensus on the number of new units that will be needed during a future period to replace even the currently substandard, not to mention those that are likely to become substandard during the projection period.

It would be simple enough to calculate this number and agree upon it if there were uniform building and housing codes throughout our country and if they were even as uniformly and rigidly enforced as in England. Then all units that have been declared in violation and their occupancy forbidden by local authorities could be counted and a national figure arrived at almost unanimously.

But even those municipalities and cities that have the latest codes and the best enforcement have few units at any time that are actually under the ban or in the process of demolition (except, of course, in urban renewal and redevelopment areas, and many of these are included not because of their condition, but because of conditions with which they are in close proximity and for which the local public authorities themselves are largely responsible).

And this negligence has prevailed in all our major cities ever since the first housing code was passed in this country late in the nineteenth century. The pioneers, Robert W. DeForest and Lawrence Veiller, chronicled this delinquency of public authorities in New York and several other American cities in 1903 in their two-volume, classic study, The Tenement House Problem.[1] In these volumes investigations are cited of bad housing in New York made at intervals from 1843. Far-reaching as the influence of their study has been, official adoption and enforcement of housing codes is still slack and deplorable.[2] So this method of counting substandard units is not available.

The difficulty arises from the fact that there is no generally accepted set of criteria by whose use a housing unit or group of housing units can be labeled "substandard." Anyone who has followed the trials and failures of the Bureau of the Census in its attempts to find and use such criteria understands the complexity of the task.

The efforts of the Bureau in connection with the Censuses of Housing of 1940, 1950, and 1960 have ended in its abandonment, in making the Census of Housing 1970, of the criteria used in the previous censuses. Careful,

48

concerned, and able professionals who have devoted much time and effort to the study of the experiences of the Bureau have become almost unanimous in recognizing the difficulties and in rejecting the results as beyond the bounds of reasonable error.[3]

There are a number of generalities, however, about which there is considerable unanimity of opinion.

1. The count of substandard units based on the census enumeration in 1960 of units "dilapidated" and "lacking some or all plumbing facilities" is not accurate because no two trained enumerators would rate the units in an assigned area so as to come out with the same (or almost the same) number having these traits. It is believed, however, that the numbers released by the Bureau for the Census of 1960 are on the side of understatement rather than exaggeration.

It is also almost undisputed that serious deficiencies are so subtle and frequently so concealed that their detection and rating can be objectively and uniformly accomplished only by trained engineers, architects, or public health professionals. Therefore, any number derived from use of the Census of Housing is to be taken as one that probably contains a large element of error.

2. Nor are the characteristics of the individual housing unit, or of it and the structure in which it and others are contained, the only criteria of suitability for human occupancy. The manner in which the unit is used by its occupants may determine very largely whether its occupancy may be dangerous to the health, safety, and morals of its occupants and their neighbors.

The two manifestations of this condition are overcrowding and bad housekeeping. A perfectly acceptable one-room unit, when occupied by a four- or five-person family or household may be substandard in such a use, but not in violation of any reasonable standards when occupied by only one person. The finest and best-equipped apartment, or even single-family unit, can become a hazard to its occupants and their neighborhood if it is not maintained in a state of reasonable repair (especially its plumbing and electric facilities) and of cleanliness.

3. There has come to be quite general agreement that mere age cannot be used as the sole criterion of deterioration, substandardness, or near substandardness. If the number of new units constructed since 1920, as reflected in the best statistics available on starts, is within acceptable margins of error, more than 41.4 million units have been built in that period; and their mean age is

about 24 years and the median about 21 years. And if the
average age of those standing in 1920 was the same 24
years, the average of the whole current inventory in 1970
is near 30 years--and the median 27--a span of time only
sufficient to enable them to become "housebroken."

    4. The attributes not only of the individual unit
are important to the provision of "a decent home in a
suitable environment." The house or the unit next door--
even in the next block or the same Census tract--and the
near presence of incompatible land uses may make an individual unit unacceptable. But only the crudest and most
general attempts have been made to count or estimate the
number of units that, because of their environment, should
be considered substandard.

    It is also noteworthy that public governmental agen-
cies have much more power to affect the environment than
have individual owners and managers--or the housing occupants themselves.*

    5. While there has been some serious deterioration
of the inventory in some parts of some of our large cities
during the last two decades, 1950 to 1970, many of the
worst units in the inventory immediately after World War
II have been eliminated. While the criteria used in estimating the worst units taken from the Censuses of 1940
and 1950 were not quite identical with the 1960 criteria,
and those used in 1970 not identical with the 1960 criteria, the data available from these Censuses indicate quite
clearly that the number of the worst units in the inventory has declined quite spectacularly from Census to Census.

    Using the criteria of the Census of 1950, one author-
ity estimates that in 1950 there were about 15 million
"substandard" units.[4] This number, he states, was reduced
during the decade of the 1950s by nearly 6 million units,
leaving about 11 million still standing in 1960.

    According to the Census of Housing 1970, there were
fewer than 5 million still standing that lacked any of

----

    *In view of the serious and inescapable effects of
the environment on the individual housing unit and its inhabitants, and of the emphasis in the Congressional goal
of a suitable environment, it seems a bit strange that,
in almost the next phrase of the Act of 1968, it should
be asserted that the goal could be "substantially achieved"
solely by obtaining a "sufficient" volume of new construction and rehabilitation of individual units.

the standard plumbing facilities for the exclusive use of
the occupants of the unit, and nearly three million of
these were in rural areas.[5] By whatever criteria one wants
to use, it is evident that during the 1950s and 1960s not
inconsiderable progress was made toward the elimination of
the worst units previously standing in the nonfarm stock
by the removal or rehabilitation of several million of
these units.

It will be recalled that during these two decades,
the number of nonfarm households or occupied housing units
increased by a little more than 23.5 million, but more
than 29 million new units were built. So, in addition to
providing for the increase in the number of nonfarm households, total building during the period provided some 5
million units to replace those lost by casualty, demolition, condemnation, or otherwise; and it is not unreasonable to suppose that many of these were substandard. Furthermore, the large expenditures of owners of housing units
for repairs and maintenance brought up to standard many
units previously lacking essential features and greatly
diminished the rate of depreciation and dilapidation of
those that in 1950 may have been on the borderline of
substandardness.

One is safe in saying that, though there are still
some 2 million urban and about 3 million rural units that
now lack some desirable plumbing facilities, their number
is no longer in the range in which it stood over the decades prior to 1950.

One other consideration makes it difficult to accept
the numbers needed for replacement of the substandard
that appears in the Committee's Report and in other projections, and has an important bearing upon the question
of stabilizing the residential construction industry:
vast sums have been expended, especially during the decade of the 1960s, by owners and occupants for repairs
and maintenance of the existing stock. Beginning with
1962, the Bureau of the Census has issued an annual report (except for the year 1964) giving an estimate of the
amount spent by owners and occupants of residential units
on "residential additions, alterations, maintenance and
repairs, and replacements" of their units.

According to these reports, owners of residential
units have spent on the average more than $12 billion
annually, or a total for the eight years of $98 billion
plus for these purposes. The total spent for replacement
was more than $16 billion, or $2 billion a year.

The total expenditure of $98 billion on the standing stock is more than $2.5 billion more than estimated receipts from the sale of all new single-family houses sold during the same years.* And expenditures on single-family owner-occupied houses amounted to more than 60 percent of the amount received for the new houses (see Table 4.1).

There are two significant observations that must be made about these estimates: (1) stabilization of the residential construction industry involves much more than obtaining the construction of the same (or a larger) number of new units each year; and (2) the expenditure of such a large sum on the standing stock cannot have failed to improve its quality and to eliminate deficiencies in many of its units. The total expenditure during the eight years covered is sufficient to have provided nearly $1,700 for every one of the 58 million units in the inventory in 1960.

It would seem reasonable, in addition, to assume that, if 6 million units of the inventory are to be rehabilitated for use of the lower-middle- and low-income groups, at least a third of these might be some of the 2 million urban units that were reported in 1970 to be without proper plumbing facilities or otherwise substandard or becoming substandard.[6]

In conclusion, a calm and judicious consideration of these numbers leads one to suggest that private owners of items in the existing stock may rehabilitate a larger number of units during the coming years than the Committee and the Congress called for in its mandate.

But as a matter of fact, very recent studies of the behavior of housing markets in a number of the larger metropolitan areas indicate that in the hearts of some central cities more houses are being abandoned than are being rehabilitated. And indications are that the reasons for abandonment lie more at the doorstep of municipal authorities than at that of private owners, that is, failure to provide adequate security, school facilities, sanitary services, and the like.[7] It is no longer contended, even by the most ardent supporters of public intervention in housing markets, that the provision of "a decent home in a suitable environment" can be realized by rehabilita-

---

*Except that the data on sales of new single-family houses cover all years from 1963 to 1970, while those on repairs, maintenance, and the like, begin with 1962 and omit 1964.

TABLE 4.1

Estimated Annual Expenditure of Owners of Residential
Units and of Owner-Occupants of Single-Family Units
for Additions, Alterations, Maintenance and Repairs,
and Replacements; and Estimates of Total Purchase
Price Paid by Purchasers of New Single-Family
Homes for Selected Years
(amounts in billions of dollars;
numbers in thousands)

Year	Estimated Expenditure for Repairs, etc.		Number and Total Prices Paid for New Single-Family Homes	
	Total--All	O.O.S.F.*	Number	Amount
Total	98.3	60.1	337	95.6
1962	11.0	6.0	N.A.	N.A.
1963	11.4	6.8	560	10.8
1964	N.A.	N.A.	565	11.6
1965	11.4	7.0	575	12.4
1966	11.7	7.1	461	10.5
1967	11.7	7.0	487	12.0
1968	12.7	8.1	490	13.0
1969	13.5	8.6	448	12.5
1970	14.8	9.5	485	12.9

*O.O.S.F. is an abbreviation for Owner-Occupied,
Single-Family. The total amount received from the sale
of new single-family houses is derived by multiplying the
number of homes reported sold each year by the reported
average price.

Source: Compiled and calculated from data in U.S.
Department of Commerce, Bureau of the Census, and Depart-
ment of Housing and Urban Development: Construction
Reports, "Characteristics of New One-Family Homes, 1970,"
pp. 47, 68; and U.S. Bureau of the Census, Housing and
Construction Report, Alterations and Repairs, Series H-101.

tion of existing structures alone--not even by bulldozing existing structures and building high rise "modern" facilities and making them available to the lower-middle- and low-income groups.

But the role of existing structures in a program of public intervention must be greatly strengthened, and much of the governmental contribution to housing of the poor can be more economically made by greater use of the standing stock. But this alone--whatever program or policy of government is used--must not only make greater use of the standing stock; it must, in cooperation with private markets, supplement these programs of use of housing units with others that assist immigrants from rural areas and from Mexico, Puerto Rico, and the farms of the South, in adapting to the urbanized, corporation-dominated, urban, social environment; and provide those public services such as schools, police protection, garbage removal, and public playgrounds that will enable first-generation immigrants to raise their children in this environment so that they will become law-abiding, valuable citizens rather than the leaders of revolution, drug peddlers, muggers, and murderers.

Until some such integrated social and political programs are implemented it is very nearly absurd to insist upon adoption of a specific number of units to be rehabilitated--or built, for that matter--by the use of public funds to improve the housing conditions of any income groups.

NOTES

1. Robert W. DeForest and Lawrence Veiller, The Tenement House Problem (New York: The Macmillan Company, 1903), especially vol. I, in which conditions in New York City, Buffalo, and "Leading American Cities" and in "Leading European Cities" are discussed.

2. The President's Commission on Urban Problems reported that

> a host of problems and questions arose concerning housing codes. Wide divergences of opinion exist among the code groups and governments at all levels with respect to the purpose of housing codes, how they should be enforced, and the standards they should provide.

The provisions established in the codes
for "minimum" standards of health, safety,
and welfare are often inadequate to provide
even a "minimum" level of performance for
the bulk of the population. A house can
meet the legal standards set in a local
code, pass a housing code inspection, and
still be unfit for human habitation by the
personal standards of most middle-class
Americans.

There is an obvious and urgent need for
action to bring the provisions of housing
codes up to an actual minimum level of
health (including physical, mental, and social well-being), safety, and welfare.

Our most important single finding,
however, is that minimum standards, while
enforceable, are often unenforced. Although intended to apply city-wide, the inspection of housing and the enforcement of
housing codes are frequently carried out
only in limited areas, generally excluding
both the worst and the most affluent neigh-
borhoods.

Building the American City, Report of the National Commission on Urban Problems to the Congress and to the President
of the United States (Washington, D.C.: Superintendent of
Documents, House Document No. 91-34, 91st Congress, 1st
Session), p. 274.

3. As the Bureau has expressed the problem:

The statistics should reflect the "real" as
opposed to the "apparent" state of affairs
with respect to quality of housing. This
criterion is a reflection of the fact that
the quality of a house is multidimensional.
Within the limits imposed by a nation-wide
census, any feasible system of measurement
can produce only an indication of quality,
limited in at least two respects. First, it
will certainly fail to reflect intangible,
although relevant, aspects of the quality of
a house. Second, with changes in standards,
it may fail to reflect those aspects of
quality that are regarded as important or
critical at the time the indicator is being

used. For example, one can conceive of an
indicator of quality of housing based on
the presence or absence of windows. . . .
One can conceive also of an indicator reflecting the presence or absence of air
conditioning. . . . Thus the term "real"
may be interpreted as "relevant for present
circumstances and present uses."

U.S. Department of Commerce, Bureau of the Census, "Mea-
suring the Quality of Housing: An Appraisal of Census
Statistics and Methods," Working Paper No. 25 (Washington,
D.C., 1967), p. 9. See also U.S. Bureau of the Census,
Statistical Research and Housing Divisions, "Quality of
Housing: An Appraisal of Census Statistics and Methods"
(Response Research Branch, Report No. 66-16, mimeo.)
    4. Frank S. Kristof, "Urban Housing Needs Through
the 1970's: An Analysis and Projection," Research Report
No. 10, prepared for the National Commission on Urban
Problems (Washington, D.C.: Government Printing Office,
1968), especially pp. 3-13.
    5. U.S. Bureau of the Census, Census of Housing,
1970, "General Housing Characteristics," Final Report,
HC(1)-Al, p. 54. This fact indicates another reason why
there is so much disagreement about the number of substandard units. If the presence of conditions or the lack
of facilities that endanger the "health, safety, and morals" of the occupants and their neighbors is to be taken
as the basis of such standards, then it seems unnecessary
to argue that the same criteria cannot be applied to both
urban and rural housing. When the basis is subjective and
covers the broadest interpretation of the phrase "the
general welfare," criteria become vague and uniformly in-
applicable, as is suggested by the statement of the Commission on Urban Problems when it reported that it had
found that "A house can meet the local standards set in a
local code and still be unfit for human habitation by the
personal standards of most middle-class Americans."
    6. One can only wonder why only the 6 million units
to be rehabilitated by the use of Federal subsidies should
be included in the goal while the millions that have been
improved by "alterations, maintenance and repairs, and
replacement" by current owners are ignored. One might get
the impression from this omission and from other implications found in the Hearings on the Act of 1968, and especially in the Report of the President's Committee on Urban
Housing, that one of the purposes of the provisions it

contains was to assure the building industry a steady and stabilized market for a volume of production that would almost assure its members of stabilized profits, even though this objective could be attained only by pushing the Federal government further and further into direct participation in the market.

At any rate, it was evidently this tendency that prompted Secretary Romney to testify before the House Committee on Appropriations in May 1971 that "The tab for subsidized housing is going up, and . . . the number of families [apparently he meant households] needing subsidies is increasing alarmingly." HUD _Newsletter_, May 3, 1971.

7. See, for example, the excellent study by George Sternlieb and Robert Burchell, _Residential Abandonment: The Tenement Landlord Revisited_ (New Brunswick, N.J.: Center for Urban Policy Research, 1973).

5

BUILDING TO
INCREASE VACANCIES?

The item in most of the official or semi-official projections of the needed volume of housing construction that flies directly in the face of usual market behavior is that which is intended to provide an "allowance for vacancies." In the report of the Committee on Urban Housing, this item is 1.6 million, or an annual average of 160,000 units.

Since about 20 percent of the population move every year, any proposal intended to lessen the difficulties encountered by migrants is certain to prove politically appealing. It is not desirable from the broad point of view of the whole community, it is argued, to have any impediments in the way of the household that wants to move, wherever it wants to go to, at any time it wants to go! To enable a household to do so, vacant housing units should be available from which it can choose one at a reasonable distance from places where members of the household may want to go to work or to play (though this may be impossible if the members of the household want to work or play in widely scattered places), and at prices or rents that they agree to pay, even if a part of the price or rent must be paid by the public.

It is commonly held that few vacancies of residential units impede mobility, while many, spread over a

---

I am indebted to the late Douglas V. Cannon, Economist of the Federal Home Loan Bank of San Francisco, for very helpful comments he has made on an early draft of this and the following sections. He is, of course, not responsible for any of the ideas here expressed.

wide range of prices, rents, and locations, facilitate it. This is undoubtedly true.

But it seldom if ever follows that a high vacancy rate is a mark of a healthy housing market. This contention ignores one important aspect of all housing markets: Capital resources, both private and public, are used to produce housing facilities for occupancy, not to be held vacant. Our traditional institution of private property in housing is based upon the acquisition, holding, and disposition of the legal right to occupancy and use of these capital goods, or to control their use and occupancy, in time.

Moreover, the owner of this right secures the major benefits of his ownership only when the premises are occupied and used, or when he sells his interest. Vacancy, to the private owner, nearly always represents a complete and irrecoverable loss, whether he be the owner-occupant of a single-family unit or the landlord of a multifamily structure; and to the public owner, vacancy is an irrecoverable waste of resources.

As the vacancy ratio rises, therefore, private sellers of the rights to occupancy suffer losses of income every day their unit or units lie vacant, and public sellers see another increment in the volume of wasted public resources for which they are responsible.

As a matter of fact, the single-family, owner-occupied unit in most urban communities in most transactions in the postwar period typically has not been vacated until after the rights to future occupancy were sold; and purchasers have nearly always complained that the settlement date on which they would come into the right of occupancy and possession has been so long delayed after a purchase-and-sale agreement had been signed.

Landlords of rental units try to get their sitting tenants to renew their leases, but they always reserve the right to show the premises to prospective tenants for several weeks before the term of an existing lease has expired. They do not want their units to fall vacant, except at most for a day or two while they are making repairs and redecorating. In other words, a vacant privately owned unit represents failure of some owner of the right to early possession to secure a renter or buyer before the critical day of surrendering occupancy and possession has come.

The vacancy ratio, therefore, is as much an index of success or failure of landlords and sellers to protect their estates from suffering imminent loss as it is of a greater range of choice on the part of prospective renters and purchasers. Landlords and sellers may choose to take the risk of this loss in the expectation that, after a wait, the price or rent they can get for their property will be sufficiently higher than what they can get currently to make up for it. But this, if realized, is compensation for waiting and taking the risk, not certain recovery of the amount originally asked.

A rising vacancy ratio, therefore, anticipates a declining rate of increase in rents and prices; and, if it persists long enough, and becomes deep enough, an actual fall in both. Therefore, a private seller or landlord never reduces price or rents until he becomes convinced that the consequent loss of prospective income is likely to be less than he would suffer if he stuck to his going price, prolonged the vacancy, and took the loss it brought. Falling prices and rents are a sure sign that the vacancy ratio has moved beyond the critical point where it is generally believed by sellers, builders, and landlords that the decline is likely to persist. The ratio hence usually must prevail over a period of time before private landlords, owner-occupants, and builders take the drastic step of reducing their rents or asking prices.

The data necessary to trace closely the course of vacancies, and their effects on rents and prices, and on such other market phenomena as mortgage delinquencies and foreclosures, are not generally available. But there are some series that appear to reflect the observations made above; some of these are worth citing.

The historical series on vacancies for the time period before the first Census of Housing in 1940 have to be constructed from estimates of the total housing inventory at Census dates, and the number of units in the postulated inventory, that were occupied at the time. Using the best series available, it appears that the gross vacancy rate in the nonfarm inventory was about 4.7 percent in 1890; conversely, a little over 95 percent of the units were occupied. In 1900, the situation was even tighter: about 97 percent of the inventory was occupied, leaving only less than 3 percent unoccupied.

The housing situation appears to have continued to grow tighter until 1920, when, it is estimated, over 99 percent of the units were occupied (see Table 5.1).

Construction of an estimated 7 million new units during the decade of the 1920s, and the addition of nearly one million units by other means, brought relief; and by 1930, the occupancy rate had fallen to 90.7 percent of the inventory.

TABLE 5.1

Estimated Total Nonfarm Housing Inventory, Number of Units
Occupied and Percentage Unoccupied at Census Dates 1890,
1900, 1910, 1920, 1930, 1940, 1950, 1960, and 1970; with
Total Number Classified as "Urban" and "Inside SMSA's,"
with Number Occupied and Percentage Not Occupied
at the Census Dates 1950, 1960, and 1970
(all numbers rounded to thousands)

Census Date	Total Nonfarm	Occupied	Percent Unoccupied
1890	8,319	7,923	4.7
1900	10,589	10,274	3.0
1910	14,281	14,132	1.1
1920	17,733	17,600	0.8
1930	25,692	23,300	9.3
1940	29,682	27,748	9.9
1950	39,625	37,105	6.4
Urban	29,569	28,892	3.6
Inside SMSA's	27,111	25,848	4.6
1960 Total	54,760	49,458	9.7
Urban	40,757	38,320	6.0
Inside SMSA's	36,386	34,000	6.6
1970 Total*	64,950	60,726	6.5
Urban	49,991	47,563	5.1
Inside SMSA's	46,076	43,863	5.2

*The 1970 Census of Housing gives statistics only for
"Urban" and "Inside SMSA's"; the numbers given here for
"Total Nonfarm" are estimates secured by subtracting from
the total, 67,674,000 "Year Round Housing Units," the estimate of the Bureau of the Census of 2,724,000 units
occupied in March 1970, by farm households. (Current
Population Reports, "Consumer Income," Series P-60, No.
72, August 14, 1970, p. 12.)

Other Sources: For "Total Nonfarm," 1890-1940, Leo
Grebler, Louis Winnick, and David Blank, Capital Formation
in Residential Real Estate (Princeton, N.J.: Princeton
University Press, 1956), p. 65; for other years and for
total occupied, Censuses of Housing, 1940, vol. II, "General Housing Characteristics," pp. 3, 8; 1950, vol. I,
part 1, pp. xxvii and xxviii and Table 2, p. 2. The
Bureau of the Census categories "Urban and rural nonfarm"
are not identical for the different censuses, and do not
apply to the same geographical territory; but the dis-
crepancies are not great enough to change the numbers
significantly.

Depression conditions during the 1930s brought an increase in the nonfarm vacancy ratio. The first Census of Housing, made in 1940, reported that a little less than 28 million of the 29.7 million nonfarm units were occupied; the percentage not occupied, then, was 9.9.

Notwithstanding wartime restrictions on building and the large migrations to urban areas where defense industries were located, the occupancy-vacancy ratio for the country as a whole changed less during the period 1940 to 1950 than might have been expected. The Census of Housing 1970 reported a total of 39,626,000 urban and rural non-farm units in the inventory, and 37,105,000 (93.6 percent) occupied. In urban areas, it found 29.6 million units with only 3.6 percent not occupied; and within Standard Metropolitan Statistical Areas, 95.4 percent of the units were occupied.

The building boom of the 1950s apparently brought about a reduction in the rate of overall occupancy by only a little over 2 percent, while that in congested metropolitan areas as a whole dropped by 2.4 percent.

Although the rate of building slowed up during the 1960s, the overall occupancy rate rose by the date of the Census of 1970 by only 3.2 percent, from 90.3 to 93.5 percent; in metropolitan areas by 1.4, from 93.4 to 94.8 percent (see Table 5.1).[1]

For the decade of the 1960s (and seven years of the 1950s) the Bureau of the Census has made monthly surveys and published quarterly and annual reports of vacancies (see Table 5.2). In these reports, vacancies are reported in four categories: (1) total occupied units as a percentage of the standing stock; (2) vacant units for sale for owner-occupancy as a percentage of the entire stock of units held for owner-occupancy; (3) vacant units available for rent as a percentage of the standing stock of year-round rental units; and (4) other vacancies. The last category consists of units that are temporarily vacant because of the absence of the usual occupants, sold, but awaiting occupancy, and the like.

In April 1950, according to these reports, 93.1 percent of the total inventory was occupied, with 2.5 percent "seasonal" vacant; and 4.4 percent year-round vacant. And 3.3 percent of the total stock were reported as "year-round vacant, sound or deteriorating."

In 1960, this report indicated that 89.9 percent of the total inventory was occupied, total unoccupied 10.1 percent, with 2.7 percent of the inventory vacant "seasonal," and 1.1 percent "dilapidated." Other vacancies stood at 6.3 percent.

TABLE 5.2

Estimated Vacancy and Occupancy Rates for Housing Units at Selected Dates

| Year | Percent Occupancy | Vacancy Rates | | | |
		Total	Seasonal	Dilapidated	Net Vacancy
1950[a]	93.1	6.9	2.5	1.1	3.3
1955[b]	91.7	8.3	2.4	1.2	4.7
1956	91.7	8.3	2.7	1.1	4.5
1957	91.0	9.0	3.1	1.2	4.7
1958	90.9	9.1	3.0	1.1	5.0
1959	90.9	9.1	2.6	1.2	5.3
1960	89.9	10.1	2.7	1.7	6.3
1961	90.3	9.7	2.9	0.8	6.0
1962	90.0	10.0	2.7	0.8	7.5
1963	89.7	10.3	2.8	0.7	7.8
1964	89.8	10.2	2.8	0.6	7.8
1965	89.5	10.5	2.9	0.7	6.9
1966	89.7	10.3	2.8	0.7	6.8
1967	90.1	9.9	2.7	0.7	6.5
1968	90.7	9.3	2.6	0.7	6.0
1969	90.9	9.1	2.6	0.6	5.9
1970	91.2	8.8	2.5	--	6.3
1971	91.3	8.7	2.3	--	6.4
1972	91.3	8.7	2.3	--	6.4
1973[a]	91.5	8.5	2.2	--	6.3
1974[a]	91.0	9.0	2.4	--	6.6

[a]Census of Housing, 1950.
[b]From 1955 to 1971, these numbers are taken from the Bureau of the Census, Current Housing Reports, "Housing Vacancies," Series H-111-71-5 (annual), March 1972, and from HHFA and HUD Annual Reports and Statistical Yearbook.

The occupancy rate, according to these reports, declined steadily until 1965, when it stood at 89.5 percent;
vacancy was at 10.5, with 2.9 percent reported as seasonal,
and 0.7 percent as dilapidated, leaving 6.9 percent vacant,
not counting seasonal and dilapidated.

The occupancy rate rose steadily from 1965 to 1972,
when it stood at 91.3 percent of the standing stock. The
gross vacancy rate was, therefore, 8.7; 2.3 percent of the
vacancies were seasonal; the "dilapidated" category was no
longer reported.[2]

It is impossible to interpret these ratios in terms
of their significance as an index of the relationship between market demand and supply. The Census Bureau series
for the 1950s and 1960s provides details that were not
available until that series was begun; the overall ratios
given for the census dates prior to 1940 contain so large
an element of estimate that it is questionable whether
they are comparable with those given for the subsequent
Census of Housing dates. But they are of interest and a
comparison of the entire series may be helpful in inter-
preting market conditions.

The first and most striking comparison is this: The
rate of occupancy of the nonfarm inventory was at a low
point in 1890, when it stood at 95.3 percent; and it remained above this point until 1930, rising to over 99 percent in 1920. The percentage of the rental stock reported
"vacant and available for rent" has not fallen below 2
percent since 1957; and it was above 7 percent from 1961
to 1967, since when it has been close to 5 percent. If
vacancies called "seasonal" and "dilapidated" are deducted
from the gross vacancy rate, the "net" vacancy stands at
over 6 percent for the two years, 1960 and 1961; at 7 percent or more from 1962 to 1964; at 6 percent or more from
1965 to 1968; at 6.2 from 1969 to the first quarter of
1972, and at 6.6 in the first quarter, 1973 (see Table 5.2).

These occupancy rates and the reverse ratios are frequently quoted as measuring the "range of choice" of the
homeseeker. But this interpretation is open to question;
the homeseekers' choices are found in those units which
"come on the market" over a period of time, not those for
which no occupant is found before current occupants move
out.[3]

There are two market phenomena that are closely related to the changes in these vacancy ratios, and which
are certainly critical to understanding the behavior of
housing markets: the rate of "turnover" or change in
occupancy of housing units, and the rate of delinquencies
and foreclosures of mortgages on homes.

According to the Census of Housing 1970, of the 40 million households then living in their own homes, 4.3 million, or 10 percent, reported they had moved into them during the 15 months preceding the Census date, April 1970. Exactly 50 percent, approximately 20 million, reported that they had moved into their units during the year 1965 or later. That is, half the occupied homeowner inventory had turned over in those five years.

Renters, of course, have shorter tenancies than homeowners; 40 percent of these (9.4 million) reported they had moved into their units within the 15 months preceding the census date. That is, for 40 percent of the inventory occupied by renters in 1970, occupancy had been acquired in the 15 preceding months or less (see Table 5.3), and assuming that the moves were spread evenly over the months, the average tenancy had lasted for 7.5 months.

Altogether, then, during the 15 months preceding the census date, 13.6 million, or a monthly average of roughly 900,000 households, had secured and exercised their rights of occupancy and possession of the unit they occupied at the time of the census.

But the census reported that only 4 million units were vacant at the time it was made. The households who were looking for a place to lay their heads and cook and eat their meals had, during the 15 months preceding the census date, a choice of not only many of the 4 million units reported still vacant but of the nearly 14 million additional units--a total of 17.6 million--to choose from. Assuming that these changes in occupancy were evenly distributed by months, the choice of households seeking homes in any month during the year 1969 was between approximately a million units that were "on the market" because someone wanted to get out or had already done so.[4] Contemplating these numbers, one can only wonder why the President's Committee and the officials of HUD insisted that a minimum of 160,000 (or 144,000) should be "constructed" each year for a decade to bring about an "increase in vacancies."

Valuable--indispensable--as the Bureau of the Census' vacancy series is, it cannot be taken as a measure of the range of homeseekers' choices. But it can be taken as a signal of market conditions for new construction that is being put on the market at current prices and rents. Over the whole postwar period, when the gross occupancy ratio for any major portion of the markets of the nation, reported by the Bureau of the Census, has fallen below 94 or 95 percent of the inventory, private markets have responded by a reduction of the volume of production.[5]

TABLE 5.3

Estimated Length of Tenure of All Reporting Households and of Owner-Occupants
and Renters in 1970
(numbers in thousands)

Year Moved in	Median* Months of Occupancy	Total		Owner-Occupants		Renters	
		Number	Percent	Number	Percent	Number	Percent
Total	—	63,445	100	39,885	100	23,560	100
1969 to March 1970	7.5	13,660	21.5	4,288	10.7	9,372	39.7
1968	21.0	6,385	10.0	3,083	7.7	3,312	14.0
1967	33.0	4,539	7.1	2,463	6.2	2,076	8.8
1965 and 1966	51.0	7,274	11.4	4,552	11.4	2,722	11.5
1960 to 1964	81.0	10,574	16.6	7,729	19.3	2,845	12.0
1950 to 1959	171	11,529	18.1	9,675	24.1	1,854	7.8
1949 or earlier	291	9,473	14.9	8,094	20.3	1,379	5.8

*Assuming that moves were evenly distributed over the months of the year.

Source: U.S. Bureau of the Census, Census of Housing, 1970, "Housing Characteristics for States, Cities and Counties," Part 1, U.S. Summary, vol. L, p. 248.

One other observation regarding the vacancy ratio must be mentioned. It is sometimes inferred in discussing this ratio and its meaning in housing markets that the market supply consists of all the units in the inventory; and that demand encompasses all the "demanding units" (households) in being as well as those actively looking for a unit, possession of which can be secured at once or in the very near future.

Of course, this is not the case. The owner-occupied house whose occupants intend and expect to stay in it and use it indefinitely is no more a part of the market supply than is the suit of clothes worn by the head of the household or the new automobile which he expects to drive for the next two or three years, or the rump roast that's in the freezer. And the rented unit, whose tenants expect to stay in it indefinitely, cannot "come on the market" until they or their landlord decide not to renew a lease which is about to expire.

The market "supply" consists, not of all the units in the inventory, but only of those the occupancy and use of which can be secured because they are actually, or are about to become, available for occupancy. And, similarly, market demand for the right of occupancy consists not of the total number of households in being or about to be set up, but only of those that are not in possession or have not acquired but are actively seeking the right to come into possession of a unit in the reasonably near future.

The reason for insisting upon this distinction is that failure to do so distorts the picture of the way in which changes in market demand affect market supply, and vice versa.

It is a commonplace observation that for most reproducible goods, an increase in demand brings rising prices, and rising prices bring an increase in market supply; that, conversely, a falling demand brings falling prices, and falling prices bring a decrease in the market supply.

These or similar relationships between market demand and supply may dominate housing markets in the very long run; that is, over a period of years. But few homeseekers can wait years for a place to lay their heads; and in the short run of many weeks or months, exactly the reverse appears to be typical of the behavior of housing markets. In these markets, an increase in demand, of course, tends to bring rising prices and rents; and a falling off of demand eventually brings about a decline in prices and rents.

But rising prices and rents, instead of bringing about an early increase in the market supply (as distinguished from the inventory) of housing units, actually tend to reduce it. Renters, realizing that if on expiration of the term of their current leases, they lose the right to continue in occupancy, they will have difficulty finding another unit of which they can obtain possession at the rent that they are currently paying (after they have paid their moving expenses) may haggle with their current landlord over a proposed rent increase; but they hesitate to let their rights to occupancy expire. And a much larger portion than usual "sign on the dotted line" to prevent the landlord from renting their unit "out from under them."

Likewise, owner-occupants, realizing that only with difficulty will they find an alternative place in which to live and only at the higher level of prices represented by what they could get for the units they own and occupy, hold on, write up (in their minds) the value of the equity they have acquired in their unit, and enter it in the market only if they have to move or for some other compelling reason beyond their control. And the number of units actually on the market shrinks to lower and lower levels.

Thus the market supply actually tends to shrink rather than to expand when prices and rents are rising. Except, perhaps, in the long run; over the span of years rather than months, if the excess of market demand over market supply persists, as evidenced by continuously rising prices and by fewer and fewer vacancies, and smaller and smaller turnover rates, builders and developers, becoming convinced that the trend toward higher prices and rents will continue at least for the period of time required for developing and placing new units on the market, begin these processes and eventually place their newly developed units on the market—pricing them at as much above the market price (when they are announced) as they think they can get! But the time interval between the beginning of the price rise and the completion of a sufficient number of new units to make a difference in the demand-supply relationship is so great that the family or household searching for somewhere to live, simply can't wait.

Conversely, when vacancies, mortgage delinquencies, and unsold or unrented units begin to accumulate, the smart property manager knows that he may have to reduce rents to hold sitting tenants and pull others from his competitors; the prescient owner-occupant (or the broker who advises him), comes to believe that in the reduction of the asking price is his only hope of getting a quick sale, and that the longer the sale is postponed, the lower the asking price will have to go. All "forced" sellers—

those who are obliged to sell because they are transferred, they can't meet their mortgage debt service, or their family has been dissolved--these unwilling sellers jump into the market and the units whose occupancy becomes immediately available "flood the market."

But it takes a long time for these forces to work themselves out and for their significance to become observable and convincing. Hence, building to increase the supply and slowing up the rate of building to prevent an excess of vacancies are frequently delayed until the market is in deep distress.

This observation, as well as understanding of housing markets, suggests that the only agency that can insist upon building to increase the vacancy ratio for any purpose must be a public agency that can contemplate the resultant idleness of the resource created by "overbuilding." And to see its purpose realized, it must be prepared to submit to the economic and financial loss which that overbuilding constitutes. In short, only by public subsidies (most of which will go to the building industry) can any volume of production be anticipated to increase the volume of vacancies.

NOTES

1. For both 1960 and 1970, see U.S. Bureau of the Census, Census of Population and Housing, 1970, "U.S. Summary: General Demographic Trends for Metropolitan Areas 1960 to 1970; PHC (2)" (Washington, D.C.: Government Printing Office, 1971).

2. The "rental vacancy rate" for the first quarter of 1974 is given as 6.2, and "homeowner vacancy rate" as 1.2 percent. The corresponding rates for 1973 were 5.7 and 1.0 percent. For the same time period, the "year-round vacant" rate was 6.6 in 1974 and 6.3 percent in 1973. U.S. Bureau of the Census, Current Housing Reports: Housing Vacancies, "Vacant Units in the United States, First Quarter, 1974," Series H-11-74-1, Issued May 1974.

3. Several years ago, it was forcefully indicated that the vacancy rate indicates only "the prevalency of available housing at a given moment in time," and does not indicate what range of choice the homeseeker has over a period of time. This important datum can be obtained only from a record of turnover, that is, changes in occupancy. See Robert C. Schmitt, "Mobility, Turnover, and Vacancy Rates," Land Economics 33 (August 1957) 3:261.

4. But, since moves are not distributed evenly through the year, and movers do not ordinarily "shop" for a home for a whole year, the movers cannot take advantage of all the units that come on market during that period of time.

The Annual Report of the Department of Research of the National Association of Real Estate Boards entitled "1971 Existing-Home Sales Series" indicates that during that year, for every 100 existing homes reported sold during the months of December, January, and February, 154 were sold during the summer months of June, July, and August (Washington, D.C.: National Association of Real Estate Boards [not dated]), p. 1.

But the illustration still serves to make clear the point that the vacancy situation at a given moment or day does not give an accurate picture of the movers' choices, either.

5. It must be noticed that in an appeal to the Supreme Court of the Commonwealth of Pennsylvania of a decision of the lower courts holding that with a "mean habitable vacancy rate for the city of Philadelphia" that had "increased from 1.3 percent . . . to 3.4 percent there was in that city no emergency housing shortage . . . which would have justified the enactment of the rent control ordinance." The lower court accepted the evidence of the Director of the Philadelphia Housing Association, who, it was informed, if called as a witness, would testify that "5% is the normal vacancy rate but that 5% . . . probably had never been the normal vacancy rate in Philadelphia; that she thought . . . it would probably fall somewhere under five and above three. . . ." (387 Pa. 362).

When the rate of occupancy reported quarterly by the Bureau of the Census from 1955 to date is converted to a five-quarters moving average, centered on the third quarter, the average moved downward from 91.5 percent in the last quarter of 1955 to a low of 89.9 for the first quarter of 1960 and stays at or below 91 until the fourth quarter of 1966. Then it stays below 91 until the third quarter of 1969 and fails to reach as high as 92 through 1972.

The report for the second quarter of 1974 indicated an occupancy rate of 90.7, representing a decline of 0.5 percent from 91.2 in the second quarter for 1973.

6

DELINQUENCIES, FORECLOSURES, AND UNSOLD INVENTORY

Availability and periodic cost of funds borrowed on mortgage have become important criteria of the ease or difficulty of selling new houses; and mortgage lenders become more and more cautious and stingy with their funds as debtors to whom they have previously lent on mortgage security become less prompt in meeting their obligations; delinquencies reflect this tardiness of previous borrowers, and foreshadow less and less willingness of lenders to commit further amounts in a market when delinquencies are rising. Delinquencies also foreshadow harsh treatment of delinquents that eventuates in resort of the lender to the traditionally heartless action of foreclosure.

When delinquencies are rising, therefore, the seller of houses finds it nearly impossible to get firm commitments from the lending institution to finance the sale for the seller, especially if he is accustomed to building on a large scale measured in numbers of houses built in a single season. The hesitancy of lenders to make many commitments naturally follows the accumulation of delinquencies; and the volume of new construction projected by the builder depends in many instances on the number of units for the sale of which he can secure advance commitments from his usual sources of mortgage money.

But all builders are not so tied to their lenders' apron strings that they confine their building program precisely to the number for which they can secure firm commitments; some of them drive on, testing the market as best they can as building proceeds, and take the chance that they can dispose of their product when it is ready. But these are few, and not many of the few are likely to

schedule as large a volume of new building as they would
if they could be surer of financing their sales when the
buildings are far enough along to intrigue a buyer.
Hence, when the lender becomes cautious and stingy, the
volume of projected building as well as the number of new
units actually started is likely to decline; and even the
smaller number projected may accumulate, unsold, in the
hands of the builder.

The rate of delinquencies, and their successor, foreclosure volume, therefore, are at the core of vital statistics as far as the housing industry is concerned.   It
is important to examine next the available statistics that
reflect these influences on the building industry and have
so great a bearing on the volume of new construction.

There is only one series of foreclosure statistics
that extends back to the years before World War II--an
estimate of the number of nonfarm foreclosures published
by the Federal Home Loan Bank Board, beginning with 1926.
In that year the Board estimates that there were 61,000
foreclosures; in 1927, 91,000; and in 1928, 116,000.
Since their volume rose so precipitously during these
years, it seems safe to assume that their upward trend
began before 1926--the year when the volume of construction of new housing units reached its peak and stood at
937,000.   This volume of construction declined rapidly
after 1928.

This series of foreclosures reached its pre-World
War II peak in 1933, when their number is estimated to
have been 252,000.   It was in that year that the Home
Owners' Loan Corporation intervened in the market to reverse this upward movement, and the number of foreclosures
declined at almost as rapid a rate as that at which it had
risen.[1]   By 1946 it had fallen to 10,000.

This series remained at a low level until 1953.   In
that year it began a very steep rise that brought it to
more than 100,000 foreclosures by 1964.   It remained
above this number through 1971, with the single exception
of the year 1969, and for the year 1973 it stood at
136,000.   The years of the steepest rises were 1961 to
1962, 1957 to 1958, and 1952 to 1954 (see Table 6.1).*

----

*The series was corrected in the late 1960s, and
the new series shows a decline from 101,000 in 1968 to
96,000 in 1969 and a rise back to 101,000 in 1970, and
136,000 in 1973.

TABLE 6.1

Number and Rate of Foreclosure of Nonfarm Mortgages
and of Mortgages in the Portfolios of Insured
Savings and Loan Associations, 1946-73

Year	Nonfarm Mortgages		Insured Savings and Loans	
	Number	Rate	Number	Rate
1946	10.5	n.a.*	n.a.	n.a.
1947	10.6	n.a.	n.a.	n.a.
1948	13.1	n.a.	n.a.	n.a.
1949	17.6	n.a.	n.a.	n.a.
1950	21.5	2.17	n.a.	n.a.
1951	18.1	1.67	n.a.	n.a.
1952	18.1	1.55	n.a.	n.a.
1953	21.5	1.70	n.a.	n.a.
1954	26.2	1.93	n.a.	n.a.
1955	28.5	1.94	n.a.	n.a.
1956	40.0	1.97	n.a.	n.a.
1957	34.2	2.08	n.a.	n.a.
1958	42.4	2.46	n.a.	n.a.
1959	44.1	2.44	n.a.	n.a.
1960	51.4	2.71	n.a.	n.a.
1961	73.1	3.70	n.a.	n.a.
1962	86.4	4.18	n.a.	n.a.
1963	98.2	4.52	42,953	5.05
1964	108.6	4.79	49,076	5.44
1965	116.7	4.93	53,788	5.70
1966	117.5	4.81	55,729	5.76
1967	110.5	4.38	47,435	4.83
1968	90.9	4.01	32,512	3.24
New Series				
1967	134.2	5.05	48,220	4.92
1968	110.4	4.01	32,512	3.24
1969	95.9	3.37	21,535	2.09
1970	101.1	3.44	19,493	1.86
1971	116.7	3.80	20,464	1.89
1972	132.3	4.11	22,958	1.99
1973	135.8	4.05	n.a.	n.a.

*Not available.

Sources: Historical Statistics, Savings and Loan
Fact Book; HUD Statistical Year Book and FHLBB Journal.

There are seven other statistical series of these critical market phenomena: (1) the number and rate of delinquencies of mortgages insured by the FHA; or (2) the number and rate of foreclosure of mortgages insured by the FHA, or (3) guaranteed by the Veterans Administration; (4) the number and rate of foreclosures of mortgages in the portfolios of insured savings and loan associations; (5) the rate of delinquency and foreclosure rates of mortgages serviced by formerly about 400 and currently about 800 members of the Mortgage Bankers Association of America; (6) delinquency and foreclosure rates on mortgages held in the portfolios of reporting life insurance association companies; and (7) an unpublished series of mortgage delinquency and foreclosure rates on mortgages held by reporting mutual savings banks.*

The story of delinquencies on FHA-insured mortgages begins with the year 1950. At the end of that year, there were 1,512,000 mortgages in force, of which just over 17,000 were delinquent; thus there were only 11.3 mortgages delinquent for every 1,000 in force. The number delinquent increased in 1951 but the rate declined; both number and rate declined in 1952 and 1953. At the end of the year 1953, 10,800 were delinquent, and these represented only 5.6 per thousand in force.

At the end of the year 1954, the number delinquent had risen to over 16,000, and the delinquency rate to 8.1 per thousand. For another three years, 1955, 1956, and 1957, both series declined and in 1957 only 10,300 (4.5 per thousand in force) were in default. The rate of decline in defaults was some 44 percent. From 1954 to 1957, the number in force had risen by more than 300,000 or 15 percent; but the number in default had declined by nearly 6,000.

---

*The rate of default is the number in default per 1,000 in force, for both the FHA and the VA; the rate of foreclosures of mortgages insured by the FHA or guaranteed by the VA is the number foreclosed per 1,000 insured or guaranteed. The rate of default of mortgages serviced by members of the Mortgage Bankers Association is the percentage of the total number of mortgages of the type held and serviced by the reporting members reported as in default on the mortgages held by life insurance companies, the rate of default is the percentage of the total amount invested in these various types of mortgages.

74

From 1958 to 1965, both the number and the rate of default rose every year; in 1965, more than 64,000 were in default--15.7 for every thousand in force. But in 1966 again both the default rate and the number in default declined; and the rate continued to decline until the year 1968, when it reached the level of 13.5 per thousand in force. The rate declined again in 1969, but rose from 14.8 to 18.4 per thousand in force in 1970; to 22.6 in 1971; and 27.5 in 1972 (see Table 6.2).

TABLE 6.2

Number and Rate of Delinquencies at Year End of
FHA-Insured Home Mortgages, 1950-73
("Rate" is the number in default
per 1,000 in force)

| Year | In Default | | Year | In Default | |
	Number	Rate		Number	Rate
1950	17,058	11.3	1962	46,186	13.3
1951	18,007	10.9	1963	55,551	14.1
1952	10,562	5.9	1964	59,611	15.4
1953	10,778	5.6	1965	64,018	15.7
1954	16,231	8.1	1966	60,368	14.2
1955	14,988	7.0	1967	63,184	14.4
1956	11,973	5.4	1968	61,604	13.5
1957	10,333	4.5	1969	70,832	14.8
1958	14,455	5.6	1970	93,005	18.4
1959	16,970	5.9	1971	120,618	22.6
1960	26,850	8.7	1972	148,614	27.5
1961	40,713	12.3	1973	121,753	--

Sources: For the years 1950-61, Hearings before the Subcommittee on Housing of the Senate Committee on Banking and Currency, 88th Congress, 2nd Session, January 27 and 28, 1964, on "FHA Mortgage Foreclosures," pp. 218, 219; 1962 to 1964, HHFA Annual Reports, "Default Status of FHA Insured Mortgages"; 1965, HUD Annual Report, p. 73 (where many of the series 1950 to 1965 are also given); 1966 to 1970, HUD Statistical Yearbook, 1970, p. 203; and 1971-73, mimeo. Report of HUD, as of December 1973.

By the criterion of rate of default, the years 1950, 1954, and 1965 were the most critical for the FHA prior to the 1970s. For these were the years when the peaks of default ratio were reached. The years when it was at trough were 1953, 1957, and 1968. At the peak of 1954 the percentage of loans in default was nearly 45 percent greater than when it was at the trough of 1953; and at the peak of 1965, the rate was some 80 percent higher than at the trough of 1957. The rate of decline from the peak in 1954 to 1968 was about 14 percent.

It is disturbing to note that at the end of the year 1972, 149,000 (2.75 percent or 27.5 per thousand of those in force) were in default; and at the end of the year 1973, the number seriously delinquent exceeded 121,000 (see Table 6.2).

The Mortgage Bankers Association of America has published a series of reports of delinquencies of home mortgage loans serviced by about 400 (now 700) reporting members. These reports, published quarterly since 1953, give the percentage of all home mortgage loans serviced by reporting members throughout the United States that are delinquent. Statistics are given for those that have any delinquency, those delinquent for only 30 days, 60 days, and 90 days, and those that are in foreclosure. They also give these rates for the three types of home mortgage loans represented in members' servicing portfolios; namely, FHA-insured, VA-guaranteed, and conventional. The reports also give separate numbers for several geographic regions of the United States.

In the early years the number of mortgages in these portfolios was estimated to be more than 4.5 million; and currently they are believed to represent about $85 billion of mortgage debt.

The reports are made as of March 31, June 30, September 30, and December 31 of each year. It is evident from a casual glance at the series that there is a definite seasonal effect in their behavior; the numbers as of December 31, the last quarter of the year, are consistently higher than those for other quarters.

But, since the numbers reported by the FHA are only for the end of the year, analysis of the two series, based solely on the numbers for the last quarter of the year, may prove to be quite satisfactory. In comparing them, it must be noted, also, that the numbers given by the FHA are of mortgages "in serious default," which probably means in default for 60 or 90 days. Those given by the MBA include all loans upon which there is any payment overdue for 30 days (see Tables 6.2 and 6.3).

TABLE 6.3

Percentage of One-to-Four-Family Mortgage Loans
Serviced by Members of MBA Reported in Default
at Selected Year Ends by Type of Mortgage

Year	Total	VA	FHA		Conventional
1959	2.34	2.16[a]	1.60[a]		1.13[a]
1960	2.81	2.47[a]	1.95[a]		1.21[a]
1961	3.10	3.74[b]	3.08[b]		1.85[b]
1962	3.04	3.53	2.65		1.21
1963	3.30	3.79	3.49		1.38
1964	3.21	3.61	3.45		1.87
1965	3.29	3.60	3.59		1.87
1966	3.40	3.59	3.77		2.05
1967	3.47	3.61	3.89		1.98
1968	3.17	3.21	3.63		1.80
1969	3.22	3.15	3.75		1.75
1970	3.64	3.46	4.30		1.94
1971	3.93	3.52	4.74		2.12
1972	4.65	4.20	5.83		2.48
			EX[c]		
1973[e]	4.70	4.34	3.77[c]	14.71[d]	2.57
1974 (March 31)	4.01	3.66	4.25[c]	11.68[d]	2.55

[a]Percentage of loans delinquent on one payment only.

[b]Percentage from this date of loans with any delinquency.

[c]Excluding loans insured under the provisions of Sections 235 and 237.

[d]Percentage of delinquencies of loans insured under the provisions of Sections 235 and 237 only.

[e]The National Delinquency Survey was revised and enlarged in 1973, and since December of that year "analyzes over 6.4 million mortgage loans on 1- to 4-family residential properties, totalling an estimated $87 billion of debt. They represent more than one out of every four outstanding single-family mortgage loans in the nation, and over one half of all FHA and VA loans in force. These loans are serviced by more than 700 MBA members reporting in the survey," according to the announcement in the survey dated December 1973.

In both series, it will be noticed, two distinct cycles have occurred since 1954: In the first cycle, the delinquency rate falls from 1954 to the end of 1956--in two years--and rises from 1956 to 1964; the rise in these eight years is of the magnitude of nearly 50 percent.

From 1965 to 1968 the rate falls approximately 7 percent, and rises from 1968 to the latest date reported, when the MBA series reached the highest point ever recorded, and the FHA followed suit with more than 121,000 borrowers in arrears.

One of the most striking features of this whole series issued by the MBA is the wide difference between the rate of delinquency reported on government guaranteed and conventional mortgages. Throughout the whole period 1953 to 1972 the rate suffered on mortgages guaranteed by the VA and serviced by members of the MBA varied from 1.96 to 1.64 times that realized on conventionals. Similarly, a larger proportion of FHA-insured were in default from 1958 to 1972. In 1972, the rate on FHA loans was seriously affected by defaults on loans insured under the provisions of Sections 235 and 237; but these are shown separately by the MBA report; and on all other insured loans, the FHA rate of delinquency was at a disturbing height in 1972. The disparity between these two types of government-assured loans and conventionals is, of course, partially accounted for by the fact that MBA members have reportedly made few high ratio (of loan to value) conventional loans.

Delinquencies, however, are but portents of the catastrophe of foreclosure; and the higher the rate of delinquencies, the more serious the catastrophe which they portend. Hence, it becomes necessary to take a look at the record of FHA and VA foreclosures. Fortunately, this record is available from 1948 to 1973; and, like delinquencies, the rate of failure is more enlightening than the number (both are given in Table 6.3).

Before we take a look at the behavior of the rate, it is worthwhile to get a view of the magnitude of the financial reverse that struck about 1963, and continues to take its toll, even into the decade of the 1970s.

During the whole decade of the 1950s, foreclosures of both the FHA and the VA totaled 81,000, or an annual average of about 8,000. But during a stretch of only five years, from 1963 to 1967, more than 331,000 of these government-guaranteed or insured loans met disaster. And during the whole period of 21 years--1950 to 1970--Uncle Sam took title (or deed in lieu) to more than 656,000 homes, and thereby became the largest dealer in homes and the largest residential landlord in this country, and probably in the world.

The rate of foreclosure is unique for each of these government agencies. For the FHA, the lowest rate came in 1951, when this action was taken against one mortgage for every 1,000 in force; in 1965 and 1966, action was taken against 12 for every thousand in force. In 1972, 63,500 were foreclosed by both FHA and VA, and the rates of both reached the unprecedented heights of 3.22 for the VA and 9.51 for FHA (see Table 6.4). Previous peaks in the FHA rate came in 1956 and 1965. FHA troughs came in 1953, when less than one per thousand was foreclosed and in 1958 when the rate dropped to 1.53 from 2.46 per thousand the year before; and in 1969 when the rate was just about half what it had been in 1956 and 1957.

The peaks and troughs of the VA experience were timed nearly the same as those of FHA, except that the little wiggle in the FHA experience in 1957 and 1958 did not appear in the record of the VA; it passed from a trough of 0.11 per thousand in 1952 to 6.72 in 1964, by rather small increases in the rate every year until 1960, and then by larger steps that varied from 0.48 to 1.56 per thousand. The largest step occurred from 1961 to 1962. For the year 1972 the VA rate stood at 3.22, with the FHA rate at 9.51.*

According to the reports of the Home Loan Bank Board, the number of nonfarm mortgage foreclosures rose from 10,500 in 1946 until 1950, when they numbered 21,500. The rate of foreclosure (the percentage of all nonfarm mortgages in force) stood in 1950 at 2.17. Both the number and the rate rose (with one exception for the rate) until 1967, when a new series was introduced. The new series fell from 134,200 and a rate of 5.05 in 1967, to 95,900 and a rate of 3.37 in 1969, whence both series

---

*One reason for the disparity, of course, is that the number of new loans guaranteed by the VA had been declining, while those on the books had been maturing, that is, reaching the ages during which the expected rate of delinquency and foreclosure almost invariably decline. The FHA was increasing the number outstanding, many of which had been insured under conditions that almost assured an increased rate of trouble, as has recently been deplored in many large cities in connection with loans insured under Section 235. But the change in direction is significant.

TABLE 6.4

Number of FHA- and VA-Insured or Guaranteed Home
Mortgages Foreclosed (or Deed in Lieu Received)
by Years, 1950-72, with Foreclosure Rate
(number foreclosed per 1,000 in force)

Year	Total	FHA	VA	Rate FHA	Rate VA
1950	7,065	2,610	4,455	2.00	2.92
1951	4,126	1,523	2,603	1.01	1.33
1952	4,049	1,478	2,571	.89	.11
1953	3,590	1,132	2,458	.63	.98
1954	6,249	3,451	2,834	1.77	1.04
1955	7,740	4,021	3,719	2.00	1.24
1956	10,542	5,268	5,274	2.46	1.53
1957	10,111	3,405	6,706	1.53	1.58
1958	12,124	3,087	9,037	1.34	1.38
1959	15,866	5,233	10,643	2.03	2.95
1960	20,384	9,332	11,052	3.25	2.86
1961	36,778	20,718	16,060	6.70	4.19
1962	53,685	31,825	21,860	9.65	5.75
1963	61,048	37,863	23,185	10.89	6.24
1964	67,557	49,982	24,575	11.80	6.72
1965	69,779	46,624	23,155	12.08	6.46
1966	72,070	49,205	22,865	12.03	6.47
1967	60,868	42,198	18,670	9.93	5.44
1968	49,234	34,495	14,739	7.84	4.27
1969	39,125	28,041	11,084	6.14	3.18
1970	40,847	30,403	10,444	5.99	2.93
1971	51,555	41,062	10,493	7.69	2.86
1972	63,538	51,299	12,239	9.51	3.22

Sources: From 1950 through 1969, "Housing and Development Trends," Annual Summary, May 1970, p. 56;
for 1970, 1971, and 1972, HUD Statistical Yearbook, 1972,
p. 361. Rates computed for 1970, 1971, and 1972.

have risen every year (except that the rate did not rise from 1972 to 1973). In 1972, foreclosures totaled 132,300 and represented a rate of 4.11 (see Table 6.1).

Similarly, the experience of reporting life insurance companies was that the percentage of nonfarm mortgages delinquent rose from 1955 to 1965, when it stood at 0.93 percent of their entire portfolio, declined to 0.57 by 1969, and then began another rise. It stood at 1.57 in 1973.

Here, again, the spread between the rate of delinquency on conventional and that on government-insured or guaranteed mortgages is striking (see Table 6.5).

TABLE 6.5

Mortgage Delinquency Rates,* Reported by Life Insurance Companies on Selected Types of Mortgage Investments

Year	Total Nonfarm	FHA	VA	Conventional
1955	0.58	0.62	0.83	0.44
1960	0.61	0.82	0.98	0.40
1965	0.93	1.79	1.29	0.58
1966	0.86	1.47	1.15	0.64
1967	0.80	1.41	0.98	0.61
1968	0.63	0.91	0.88	0.53
1969	0.57	0.98	0.87	0.44
1970	0.85	1.34	0.95	0.74
1971	0.90	1.65	1.00	0.74
1972	1.13	1.85	1.08	1.02
1973	1.57	1.99	0.96	1.56

*As a percentage of total amount invested.

Source: "1971 Economic and Investment Report," Life Insurance Association of America, Table 16, p. 39.

One other statistical series developed by the Bureau of the Census illuminates conditions in private housing markets throughout the country. This series is entitled "New One-family Homes Sold and For Sale." This series is available from 1963, monthly in both seasonally adjusted form and unadjusted, and in annual unadjusted form. The annual data are given in Table 6.6.

TABLE 6.6

Ratio of the Number of New Homes "For Sale"
at the End of the Year to the Total Number
Sold During the Year, 1963-73
(numbers in thousands)

Year	Number Sold	Number "For Sale"	Ratio "For Sale"/Sold
1963	560	265	.47
1964	565	256	.45
1965	575	228	.40
1966	461	196	.43
1967	487	190	.39
1968	490	218	.44
1969	448	228	.51
1970	485	227	.47
1971	656	294	.45
1972	718	416	.58
1973	620	456	.74

Source: U.S. Bureau of the Census, Construction Reports, "Single-family Homes Sold and for Sale," C25-74-2, April 1974; C25-72-10, October 1972.

According to these data, the inventory on the hands of developers at the end of the year represented from 39 to 74 percent of the total sold during the year. The former ratio prevailed in 1967, and the latter in 1973.

This ratio, nearly twice that of the year 1967 and 50 percent above that which prevailed at the previous peak of .51 in 1969, is one consequence of the campaign of the Republican regime to whip up production so as to overcome the "critical crisis" which that administration saw "throughout the country" and to achieve the quota set for it by the prestigious "interagency task force" established in its first year to reschedule the quota set for it by the Congress over the remainder of the ten-year span contemplated in the Act of 1968.

The campaign resulted in "starts" of 2,356,000 units in 1972 and 2,503,000 in 1973, and the number of homes for sale at the end of 1972, 416,000, represented 58 percent of the number sold during that year; but with 456,000 left over at the end of 1973, the ratio was 74 percent of the number sold during that year.

We now take a look at the relationships between these four series: vacancies, delinquencies, foreclosures, unsold inventory of new units, and the volume of construction of privately owned residential units.

It is evident from the statistics we have examined that the housing crisis deriving from World War II and its consequences had been largely resolved by 1955. Disregarding the 1.9 million units reported started in 1950 (see footnote p. 2) production had held steady around 1.5 million a year for six or seven years, the gross occupancy rate had fallen from 93 percent to 91.25; the FHA delinquency rate had fallen from 2.30 per thousand mortgages in force, to 1.75; and foreclosures of FHA-insured mortgages had slightly declined from 2 per thousand to 1.77.

A falling trend in gross occupancy beginning in 1955, continued for ten years, until 1965 (judged from the moving average series), with only four very slight changes in direction. But in number of units started, there was a large increase in both 1958 and 1959. At the same time, the FHA delinquency rate began an upward trend, that continued uninterrupted for the same number of years, to 1965. Finally, FHA foreclosures also turned up in 1956, continued in that direction in 1957, turned down slightly in 1958, and then began its upward movement in earnest, which was continued at a rapid pace (with the exception of the year 1961) until 1964.

Evidently, when the occupancy rate had fallen to less than 90 percent, the delinquency rate had passed 1.25, and foreclosures had risen to nearly ten per thousand--all of which occurred by 1962--the private markets of the country were fed up. For starts, that had risen steadily from a trough of 1.2 million in 1960 to a peak of 1.6 million in 1963, fell to 1.45 million in 1965, and then precipitously to 1.15 million--the lowest point in the whole postwar period--in 1968 (election year).

The FHA delinquency rate, which had reached its postwar peak in 1965, declined through 1966, and a little more slowly in 1967 but fell further in 1968.

The occupancy rate began to rise, with the slump in the number of new units coming on the markets from 1963 to 1968, and the number of FHA foreclosures, which had held at its highest postwar level from 1964 through 1966, fell continuously to 1969. And the ratio of inventory to new homes sold had risen from 3.20 in 1966 to 6.11 in 1969. Then, in that same first year of the Nixon administration, 1969, the volume of construction declined to 1.4 million.

But in 1970, all the power of the Federal government was bent upon increasing the number of units constructed (presumably for the benefit of the "lower-middle and low-income groups"), and the volume of starts began the precipitous rise that reached an all-time high of over 2.2 million units in 1972. This, notwithstanding that the rate of delinquencies in both the FHA and the MBA series, and in all the other series available to those who were concerned, was rising very rapidly, beginning the very year that the volume of starts began its spectacular rise.

Foreclosures followed suit, at a slow but ominous pace. Unsold inventory of new houses declined in 1967 and 1970, when it stood at 5.62 percent, but in the first quarter of 1971 it began an upward jump that continued without serious interruption until it had tripled by the end of 1973, the third year in which the total of starts had exceeded two million!

There must be something besides "credit crunches" in housing markets that has some influence on the number of privately owned units started each year.

NOTES

1. A thoughtful and definitive treatment of the operations of the Home Owners Loan Corporation and of their significance is found in C. Lowell Harriss, History and Policies of The Home Owners' Loan Corporation (New York: National Bureau of Economic Research, 1951).

7

OVERCROWDING AND
THE "NEED" FOR
SECOND HOMES

In projecting the volume of building necessary to meet the social needs, it is sometimes asserted, provision must be made for eliminating overcrowding of housing facilities.

In recognition of the fact that crowding too many people into too little space compels them to endure a housing situation that is not only unpleasant but may be injurious to their health, safety, and welfare, the Bureau of the Census has tried in every Census of Housing to provide materials that can be used to indicate how many households and families are overcrowded, and the intensity of their overcrowding. No satisfactory criteria of overcrowding, however, have been found.

Taking its clue from the Census of Housing of Great Britain, in its first census made in 1940 and in every subsequent census, the Bureau has used the crude index of number of persons in the household divided by the number of rooms in the dwelling unit it occupies. The number of households or units is given in five classes of ratios of persons to rooms: (1) 0.50 or less; (2) 0.51 to 0.75; (3) 0.76 to 1.00; (4) 1.01 to 1.50; and (5) 1.51 or more.

In estimating the number of overcrowded units, one takes as the dividing point whichever of these ratios he considers to be the maximum--or that ratio below which households are not overcrowded and above which they are. The ratio most frequently chosen is 1.00. Units in which there are more persons than rooms are said to be over-crowded, and the number reported by the last census in which this ratio is exceeded is added to the list of units that should be constructed to meet the social need.

According to the Census of Housing 1970, a little more than 5 million units were overcrowded, assuming that

a ratio of 1 or more persons per room signifies overcrowding (see Table 7.1). But this simple figure is not very
illuminating. For the number of rooms in year-round housing units in 1970 must have been something more than 343
million; while there were only 197 million occupants--or
if every household had been occupying one-and-a-half rooms
per person, only 275 million of these rooms would have
been occupied; about 68 million would have been unoccupied.
Even at two rooms per person in the households, only about
51 million more rooms would have been needed (see Table
7.2).

TABLE 7.1

Numerical and Percentage Distribution of Occupied
Housing Units in the United States in 1970 by
Number of Persons per Room and by Tenure
(all numbers rounded to millions; hence
details do not always add to totals)

Number of Persons	Total		Owner-Occupied		Renter-Occupied	
	Number	Percent	Number	Percent	Number	Percent
Total	63.0	100.0	39.9	62.8	23.6	37.1
0.50 or less	31.6	49.7	21.0	57.6	10.6	44.9
0.51 to 0.75	14.4	22.6	9.0	22.6	5.4	22.9
0.76 to 1.00	12.3	19.3	7.2	18.1	5.0	21.3
1.00 to 1.50	3.8	5.9	2.1	5.2	1.7	7.2
1.51 or more	1.4	2.2	0.6	1.4	0.8	3.5

Source: U.S. Bureau of the Census, Census of Housing, 1970; "General Housing Characteristics," Final Report
HC(1)-A1, p. 22.

TABLE 7.2

Numerical and Percentage Distribution of Housing Units by Number of Rooms
and of Households by Number of Persons, 1970
(numbers in thousands)

Number of Rooms or Persons	Distribution of Rooms				Distribution of Persons			
	Units		Rooms		Households		Persons	
	Number	Percent	Number	Percent	Number	Percent	Number	Percent
Total	67,657	100.0	343,414	100.0	63,450	100.0	197,339	100.0
One	1,306	1.9	1,306	0.4	11,146	17.5	11,146	5.6
Two	2,459	3.6	4,918	1.4	18,781	29.5	37,562	19.0
Three	7,570	11.2	22,710	6.6	10,909	17.1	32,727	16.5
Four	14,131	20.8	56,524	16.4	9,803	15.4	39,212	19.8
Five	16,874	24.9	84,370	24.5	6,198	9.7	30,990	15.6
Six	13,482	19.9	80,892	23.5	3,360	5.2	20,166	10.2
Seven	6,376	9.4	44,632	12.9	1,698	2.6	11,896	5.9
Eight	3,269	4.8	26,152	7.6	940	1.4	7,520	3.7
Nine or more	2,191	3.2	21,910	6.3	613	0.9	6,130	3.1
Median	5.0						3.0	

Source: Calculated from U.S. Bureau of the Census, Census of Housing, 1970: "General Housing Characteristics," Final Report, HC(1)-A1, p. 22.

If the total number of rooms in the inventory were less than the number of persons they housed, then it might be argued that more and larger units should be built to resolve this shortage. There were in the inventory in 1970 approximately 1.7 rooms per person living in households. But there were more than 11 million one-person households and only 1.3 million one-room housing units. Ten million one-person households were living in units with two or more rooms. There were only a little more than 3.2 million households of seven or more persons, but there were 11.8 million housing units with seven or more rooms. If the 26 million persons living in households of seven or more persons had been in occupancy of the housing units that had seven or more rooms, each of these occupants would have had an average of 3.6 rooms.

Obviously, the remedy for overcrowding is to make some of the underutilized units available to those households that are now living in smaller units than their number suggests they should have.

More than 5 million households were reported to be living with more than one person per room, and 1.4 million with 1.5 persons per room. But this situation was not due to a shortage of larger units or rooms; it was attributable to the fact that households were not distributed by size to housing units by size.

Some households are living in overcrowded conditions because they cannot afford the extra rent or price that ordinarily is paid for the use of larger units; some because they prefer to use their available resources to purchase other things than the right of occupancy of more rooms. What is needed to remedy or eliminate this condition is not the federal subsidization of the construction of new units, but assistance to those households that can't afford (but not to those who prefer to spend their resources on some other form of expenditure) more housing to enable them to acquire occupancy of larger existing units. If the extra cost of occupancy of larger units they need is to be met out of public funds, it would seem to be wiser public policy to determine whether that cost would be less by assisting them in securing occupancy and use of items in the existing inventory than by building larger units for their use.

In any case, it is important that the trend is rather steeply in the direction of smaller households. This trend explains why households increase more rapidly than populations; it may also have made the demand for housing much more volatile.

The second reason for omitting the number of over-crowded units in estimating the volume of new construction needed is based upon the use of the room as the unit of count. Rooms vary in size from 80 square feet of floor space to 1,000 or more. Obviously, persons occupying less than one large room each are less crowded than those using one small room each.

And provision made for carrying on the usual functions of housekeeping have an important bearing upon the crowded or uncrowded condition in which the occupants live. The luxury study one-room apartment, with its strip kitchen, its ample bathroom and closet space and its transformable bed couches, may be a much more comfortable and satisfactory home for two working persons than a three- or four-room flat.

"Room" is frequently thought of as floor space rather than as the count of the number of separate spaces into which the total floor space is divided. But there is no practical way of measuring, reporting, and tabulating floor space that can be used by those who are trying to secure an accurate statistical picture of how the households of a nation live.

It is almost a commonplace, also, that the need for space is related not only to the number of persons in a household, but also to their age and sex. A father and mother with two children of the same sex, both under the age of five, can do better with fewer rooms than can one in which the children are of different sex and both in their upper teens.

Another item included in some of the projections of volume of residential construction needed to attain the goal of the Congress is the number of units to be used as second homes--vacation or resort units, week-end houses to which the husband can retire after a four- or five-day week in town, and the like.

Reference is made in these projections to the study made jointly by the Bureau of the Census and the Department of Agriculture in 1969 on "Second Homes in the United States." This study reported that there were in the United States in April 1967 a total of 1.5 million second homes. One million three hundred thousand of these second homes were reported to be owner-occupied, and 262,000 renter-occupied. Of the 1.7 million households reported with a second home, 1.6 million were reported to own only one second home; 26,000 to own two second homes; 43,000 to rent one second home; and 9,000 were reported to own one and rent one.[1]

According to the Census of Housing 1970, 4.6 percent of the 63,445,000 households in the United States, that is, about 2.9 million, owned a second home. There is no count in the census of the number of homes owned by households that own more than one unit, nor of the number of households that own one home and rent a second home.[2]

Of the 1.7 million households reported in 1967 with a second home, nearly 1.3 million, or 74 percent, were reported to use their second home for one season only-- and 70 percent for the summer only.

Since more than 400,000 of these second homes were reported to have been built in the seven years 1960 through 1966 (with three months of 1967 included), and 35 percent of the owners or renters reported that they had acquired their second homes within the last five years, it has been commonly remarked that this market for second homes has been very rapidly expanding in recent years. It appears to have continued its expansion, especially in resort and recreation areas, well into the 1970s.

Few would disagree with these observations. But that either the market demand or the social need requires that they should be included in a quota or mandated schedule of construction "necessary to overcome the housing short-age" or to provide "a decent home in a suitable environ-ment for every American family"--even for "every American citizen in a location convenient to his work"--is a pre-mise with which many observers would heartily disagree. And it seems almost absurd to suggest that construction of the number of new units necessary to provide these must be assured even if their construction be subsidized by the use of public funds.

NOTES

1. U.S. Bureau of the Census, Current Housing Reports, Series H-121, No. 16 (Washington, D.C.: Government Printing Office, 1969).

2. U.S. Bureau of the Census, Census of Housing, 1970, "Housing Characteristics," Final Report, HC(1)-B1, United States Summary, p. 235.

This study of the Congressional quota and of the
statistical data upon which it appears to have been based
leads to the conclusion that it is unrealistic. That it
can be realized has been demonstrated by the volume of
starts (not counting mobile home shipments, as the Secretary does in his Annual Reports and as the President does
in the required Annual Reports), that has been reached
during the years 1972 and 1973.

But its realization, clearly, depends upon the extent to which governments reach further and further into
local housing markets and subsidize a larger and larger
portion of the operations of private builders.

From an examination of the statistical series that
have been used in setting the Congressional quota, it becomes obvious that one can concur, with minor reservations,
with the number suggested to provide housing units for the
probable increase in the number of households during the
decade; and, as indicated elsewhere, it seems reasonable
to take this number--13.4 million units--as needed for
this purpose, and assume that the volume that will actually be needed will lie between 10 and 13 million.

What has happened during the past two decades to
that portion of the existing stock that consisted of "substandard" units or units that were "about to become substandard," and the expenditures of owners in rehabilitat-
ing, repairing, improving, and modernizing units of the
standing stock would appear to go much further than the
proposed expenditure of Federal funds to "rehabilitate"
a minimum number of 6 million units for occupancy by
lower-middle and low-income households. It does not
seem necessary, therefore, to include this number as an

essential item in the volume of construction "necessary" to secure this volume of subsidized rehabilitation in order to provide "a decent home and a suitable environment for every American family."

It also seems clear that nothing need be added to "increase the vacancies" available to households seeking homes. This item, again, must be entered only if it is to be decided how far into the usual markets governmental agencies are to penetrate and what portion of the total market is to be taken over by their participation. Private markets cannot be expected to build to increase the vacancy ratio; and ordinary or characteristic turnover provides a large range of choice to homeseekers in most local markets in most "normal" times.

Clearly it is a contradiction in terms to hold that it is necessary to insure the availability of "second homes" to existing households in order to meet the Congressional goal.

According to these overall or global statistical series, when gross occupancy falls to less than 94 or 95 percent of the standing stock, it is also clear that the volume of new construction intended for the private markets is very likely to decline; and when the rate of delinquencies and foreclosures of mortgages on homes turns upward and pursues that course over any significant period, the volume of privately owned or ordered construction declines.

In short, so far as overall global statistics are concerned, for the foreseeable future (if any), a volume of construction of privately owned nonfarm units of 1.3 to 1.6 million units a year seems a reasonable expectation.

But all these projections based on nationwide statistics have a built-in weakness that makes conclusions based upon them suspect, however strongly they are buttressed by the most sophisticated processing. This weakness must next be examined.

THE ERROR OF AGGREGATE PROJECTIONS

The fundamental error involved in the use of aggregate statistics is that of treating "the" housing market and analyzing its manifestations as though it were directly responsive to the economic forces that assert themselves more or less uniformly throughout the nation in such statistical materials as the gross national product, "prevailing" interest rates, national employment and unemployment, national income, personal income, and changes in the indexes of the cost of living.

But there is no national housing market--not even a statewide housing market. Housing markets are ineluctably and irremediably local entities, but loosely related if at all, and almost totally unrelated so far as the market supply of housing facilities is concerned. A vacant house or apartment in Portland, Maine, can contribute nothing to the solution of a housing shortage in Portland, Oregon, or Miami, Florida.[1]

Furthermore, since the major portion of the production of new housing units is to accommodate increases in the number of demanding units (the household), the analysis of statistical relationships that have prevailed over a period in the past (even when done by a computer) can be presumed to be predictive only if it is assumed that the effects of forces that operated to cause the increases in households or potential households and their location in past years will be essentially duplicated year by year and locality by locality.

The most important of these forces to local housing markets is increase or decrease in the number of households, natural or by migration. Changes in both of these types of human behavior have been determined in the past two centuries or longer by two unpredictable, episodic societal aberrations: wars and technological advances. Neither of these can be anticipated for any significantly long future period.

Housing markets cannot be assumed to be affected indefinitely by the migratory and other demographic characteristics of people that accompany and succeed such social cataclysms as a major war, or such economic and technological developments as have been visited upon the Western world, and especially upon the United States, during the last 75 to 100 years. The effects of these episodic events become attenuated with the passage of time.

When the first transcontinental railroad was completed in 1869, for example, it served as the basis for a greatly accelerated westward migration that soon settled both rural and urban populations throughout the great West. The force of this technological development was largely exhausted by the turn of the century--certainly by the end of World War I--and by 1925, the railroads were a negligible force in determining the direction and magnitude of migrations.

The automobile had assumed the leading role as the transport means that influenced migrations; and by the end

of the 1950s or 1960s, it was a question whether the automobile had largely played out its leading part and would
give way to other means of transportation and communication.[2]

The migrations of farm labor from rural to urban
areas, set in motion by World War I, especially to large
industrial cities, and after the war, of the affluent to
winter refuge in Florida and Southern California, reached
their highest point in the middle 1920s, and by the end
of that decade were superseded by forces of depression
that reversed the flow of people, sent tens of thousands
of automobile workers from the Detroit factories back to
the hills of Kentucky and Tennessee, and dried up the
stream of refugees from the snowstorms of the North and
Central West to the sunshine and soft breezes of the
South and Southwest, for example.

If migrations came from origins and ended at destina-
tions in equal numbers and proportions, a national summary
of the number of new units that would be needed to house
migratory households would be most helpful; but they never
do.   Clearly migration is continuing in great volume into
the 1970s; but it is not having the same effect on the
number of households in the different metropolitan areas
that it had in the 1950s and 1960s.[3]

How differently these movements during the 1960s affected some of our Standard Metropolitan Statistical
Areas is of interest.   According to a recent report of
the Bureau of the Census, of the 243 Standard Metropolitan Statistical Areas reported in the Census of Population
and Housing 1970, 94 (nearly 40 percent) suffered a net
loss of population by migration from 1960 to 1970.   Some
of the areas in all size groups suffered losses (see
Tables 8.1 and 8.2).

Of the 12 largest areas, with populations in 1970 of
over 2 million for example, five suffered a net loss from
migration; and the change in the total number of persons
in these different areas, ascribable to this cause varied
from a net loss of 7 percent that came to Pittsburgh and
Boston to a net gain of 20.2 percent in the SMSA of Washington, D.C.   The largest net loss in any of the 243 areas
was in the Brownsville, Texas complex from which the
number moving out exceeded the number coming in by nearly
a third of its 1970 count.   The largest gain was 85 percent in Las Vegas, Nevada (see Table 8.1).

But those who left Pittsburgh made no housing accommodations available for any of the 20,000 households who
fled to Washington in excess of the number who escaped
from it.[4]

TABLE 8.1

Percentage of Gain or Loss in Population 1950 to 1960
and 1960 to 1970 for Selected SMSA's
(arranged in order of the greatest rate of gain)

SMSA	1950 to 1960	1960 to 1970	Population 1960 (thousands)
ost Rapidly Growing			
ort Lauderdale	297.9	85.7	620.1
aaheim, etc.	225.6	101.8	1,420
as Vegas	163.0	115.2	273
rlando	124.6	34.4	428
an Jose	121.1	65.8	1,085
dessa (Texas)	116.1	0.9	92
hoenix	100.0	45.8	968
ost Rapidly Losing			
ilkes-Barre	-11.6	-.4	342
cranton	-8.9	-0.2	234
t. Joseph	-6.5	-4.1	87
ersey City	-5.7	-0.3	609
ohnstown	-3.7	-6.4	263
exarkana	-3.1	10.4	101
neeling, etc.	-3.0	-4.0	183
ort Smith	-1.8	18.7	160
ltoona	-1.6	-1.4	135
erre Haute	-0.2	1.8	173
MSA's Losing During Both Periods:			
ilkes-Barre	-11.6	-1.4	343
cranton	-8.9	-0.2	234
t. Joseph	-6.5	-4.1	87
ohnstown	-3.7	-6.4	263
neeling	-3.0	-4.0	183
ltoona	-.16	-1.4	134
MSA's Losing 1950-60; ining 1960-70			
ort Smith	-4.8	18.7	160
erre Haute	-0.2	1.8	178
exarkana	-3.1	10.4	101
ining 1950-60; Losing 1960-70			
idland (Texas)	162.6	-0.1	114
marillo	71.6	-3.4	144
ake Charles	62.3	-0.1	145
bilene	40.8	-5.3	114
ueblo	31.6	-0.4	119
avannah	24.2	-0.3	188
ichita Falls	23.1	-1.6	130
aco	15.3	-1.7	150
aluth-Superior	9.4	-4.1	277
ittsburgh	8.7	-0.2	2,045
teubenville, etc.	6.3	-1.3	168
aarleston (West Virginia)	5.5	-9.3	253
ioux City	5.0	-3.2	120
untington-Ashland	3.7	-0.4	255
adsden	3.3	-2.9	97

Source: Calculated from U.S. Bureau of the Census, Census of Population, 1970, upplementary Report, "Population of Standard Metropolitan Statistical Areas, 1950 to 70."

TABLE 8.2

Selected SMSA's in Which Maximum Loss and Maximum Gains in Population Were
Reported for Smaller Statistical Areas in the Same SMSA*

| | 1950-60 | | 1960-70 | | |
SMSA	Maximum Loss Rate	Maximum Gain Rate	Maximum Loss Rate	Maximum Gain Rate	Population 1960
Baltimore	-1.1	82.2	-3.6	71.3	1,804
Boston	-13.3	295.4	-9.3	125.6	2,595
Bridgeport	-1.2	121.4	-0.1	88.2	338
Dallas	-4.9	54.8	0	62.2	1,119
Fort Smith	-17.5	3.9	0	29.8	135
New York	-13.4	141.5	-9.4	68.7	10,695
Providence	-16.6	46.3	-13.6	107.3	821
Terre Haute	-10.4	3.1	-8.4	5.6	172
Washington, D.C.	-4.8	170.6	-1.0	121.5	2,077

*These "smaller statistical areas" were political areas for which population
numbers were tabulated, usually incorporated places lying within the SMSA.

Source: Calculated from U.S. Bureau of the Census, Census of Population, 1970,
Supplementary Report, "Population of Standard Metropolitan Statistical Areas, 1950
to 1970."

Altogether, for the 243 Standard Metropolitan Statistical Areas, population inflow exceeded outflow by just
over 5 million. Assuming an average of 3.09 persons per
household, net gains in inflow of households exceedes loss
from outflow for these areas by just over 560,000. Assuming that these 560,000 households moved into those areas
that had net inflows of migrants, the inventories in the
149 areas that had net inflows had to be increased to provide for them; the need for additions to inventory in the
94 places that suffered net losses was reduced by the same
numbers. A calculation based upon the population changes
in the whole 243 areas would not reflect this difference
in the distribution of these 500,000 units, and would
likely be exaggerated by this number.*

Actually, total population growth by SMSA's varied
from an increase of 101 percent to a loss of 9.3 percent--
the record in Wheeling, West Virginia. One or more
SMSA's lost total population in 11 states: Colorado,
Alabama, Georgia, Iowa, Kentucky, Missouri, Minnesota, New
Jersey, Ohio, West Virginia, and Wisconsin. The maximum
rate of growth in Kansas was less than 15 percent. In
North Dakota's only SMSA, it was only 13.4 percent; in New
Jersey, just over 20 percent, in Iowa 19.2 percent; in
Minnesota, 28.3, and in Indiana, 22.7 percent. One could
almost say that the typical spread in the states in which
no SMSA actually lost population, between the lowest rate
of increase and the highest was sevenfold. Any sort of
average of numbers so widely dispersed is more likely to
be misleading than informative.

There is a similar variation in the rate of increase
in households in SMSA's (though the increase in the number
of households is invariably greater than that of the total
population). In California, the number of households in
one of its 16 SMSA's increased by 113.9 percent. But
there was one or more SMSA's in California in which the
rate of household increase was less than 13 percent; and
in Florida it was 16.1 percent.

---

*It may be remarked in passing that the importance of
this observation is more vividly realized when it is observed that these migrant households probably all took
their automobiles with them, so that a calculation of the
probable effect of migrations upon the market demand or
social need for new automobiles would not have been seriously affected by these lopsided migrations.

There was one or more SMSA's in only three states--
Minnesota, Missouri, and Wisconsin--in which the number of
households actually declined, and the decline of 1.8 percent of one SMSA in Wisconsin was the largest.

The maximum variation by states in rate of increase
in households was in Iowa; the Cedar Rapids SMSA increased
in number of households by 20.4 percent, that of Sioux
City by only 0.1 percent. In Ohio, the rate of increase
varied from 28.5 percent in the Columbus SMSA to 6.2 percent in the Steubenville-Weirton (Ohio-West Virginia) SMSA
(or 1.5 percent in the Wheeling-West Virginia-Ohio SMSA).

A similar range of variation occurs from SMSA to SMSA
by states in the report on occupancy and vacancy in the
1970 Census of Housing. Taking the nation as a whole, the
vacancy ratio for all year-round units was 6.6 percent;
but that for rental units in SMSA's varied from state to
state from a low in New York of 2.1 percent to a high of
14 percent in the Wilmington, South Carolina, SMSA. It
was more than 7 percent in one or more SMSA's in ten
states: Alabama, Arkansas, Kansas, Kentucky, Louisiana,
Missouri, Nebraska, Oklahoma, South Carolina, and Washington. And it was 5 percent or less in one or more of the
SMSA's in nine states: New York, Colorado, Massachusetts,
Ohio, Pennsylvania, Rhode Island, Utah, Virginia, and
Wisconsin.

The rental vacancy rate varied by 100 percent or more
from SMSA to SMSA in seven states: Connecticut, Florida,
Massachusetts, Michigan, New York, North Carolina, and
Pennsylvania. The homeowner vacancy ratio varied from
SMSA to SMSA within the same state by 100 percent or more
in ten states: Alabama, Connecticut, Florida, Iowa,
Kansas, Kentucky, Massachusetts, Minnesota, North Carolina,
and Pennsylvania.

The overall national vacancy ratio of 6.6 percent of
all-year-round units approximated the highest ratio for
rental units only in at least one SMSA in only four states:
Georgia, Florida, Indiana, and Iowa.

Obviously, there is no national or even statewide
vacancy ratio that can be taken as indicative of the
demand-supply relationship that actually prevails in the
nation or in a given state. And the housing market or
housing need can be estimated only with much misgiving by
taking the average of these states as a national average,
or the average for the SMSA's in a state as representative
of actual conditions in the state.

Projection of demand for local communities rests upon
interpretation of the economic conditions unique to the
community that are reflected in the critical ratios that

have been discussed.[5] But in many communities this information is not available and not enough study has been done
on how the information available should be interpreted.

A projection of the volume of new construction
"needed" to provide accommodations for increments to the
number of households anticipated for a local market quite
clearly must be based upon an estimate of the increase in
number employed or receiving earnings or other income payments; that is, of the strength and duration of the forces
that underlie the economic base of the community. It was
primarily the actions of the Federal government in con-
tracting for economic goods and services needed in the defense and war programs during the 1940s that stimulated
the migrations that so rapidly increased the population of
the SMSA's that were prepared to furnish those materials.
And after the war, it was the return of members of the
armed forces and their marriages that superimposed upon
the already crowded urban housing facilities the demand
for separate dwelling units for the households that they
wanted to establish.

These forces created at least 13 new standard metropolitan statistical areas between 1950 and 1960 in and
around cities that had not reached in 1950 the 50,000 in
population necessary to secure the appellation of SMSA.
And in the areas that had already become "grown up" by
1950, centered in our largest cities, they caused increases
in the number of households during the 1950s that numbered
more than 156,000 (103 percent) in the Miami SMSA; 206,000
(50 percent) in that centered in Washington, D.C.; 123,000
(74 percent) in Denver's; 811,000 (57 percent) in Los
Angeles'; 43,000 (45 percent) in Omaha's; 155,000 (32 percent) in St. Louis'; 133,000 (59 percent) in Seattle's;
881,000 (24 percent) in New York's; and 340,000 (21 percent) in Chicago's.

But by the end of the 1950s, the force of these influences was partly exhausted and began to subside. Then
the influence of the government's postwar space, airplane,
and other postwar defense and war material programs, and
the exploitation by private corporations of technological
developments initiated during the war, brought employment
to some of the same areas, but more to others, located at
the periphery of SMSA's or cities that had not yet become
centers of SMSA's by 1960. Only about a dozen of the 40
or 50 SMSA's that grew most rapidly in the 1950s added as
many households during the 1960s as they had added during
the 1950s.*

---

*The Bureau of the Census recently reported that the
growth in population of 21 metropolitan areas since 1970

99

The location of the hundreds of factors of thousands
of products that have become available for the first time
since 1950 has induced migrations from farms to cities,
and from the central cities to suburbs; and the provision
of services such as business consulting, medical diagnosis
and treatment, document duplication and distribution, and
advertising services of various and numerous sorts, of
television and radio program preparation and presentation--
these will suffice to suggest the impact of technological
developments, emanating from or suggested by World War II,
upon the redistribution of population that characterized
the decades of both the 1950s and the 1960s. It is not
likely that even the computer can predict the inventions
and other changes of the coming two decades that will
largely determine the volume and direction of migration
movements during that time.

In brief, the course of events accompanying and following participation in two world wars has demonstrated
that any projection of the volume of residential construction that is likely to be needed even over a short period
of future time must be constructed by the use, not of
nationwide statistics, but of series that are applicable
to small geographical areas that constitute local housing
markets.

And to be realistic, the projection must indicate
where the construction is to be located. And even then,
the longer the period of time contemplated in the projection, the wider the margin that must be allowed for un-
foreseeable shifts in consumers' preferences, the establishment and location of unborn industrial and business
units, increases or decreases in consumers' income, and
so on. The wider the margin allowed for, the greater the
confidence that can be put in the projection.

The determination of the Congress that its goal could
"be substantially achieved within . . . [a] decade . . .
by the construction or rehabilitation of twenty-six million housing units, six million of these for low and moderate income families" was made in response to the pre-
sentation of numbers arrived at by including the total
market demand for both the needed and the luxurious units
as well as the social need of families and individuals

---

had been enough to enable them to qualify as Standard Metropolitan Statistical Areas. And in these places, population grew more rapidly during these two years on the average than in the 243 SMSA's that were on the list in 1970.

who occupy units that some consider "substandard." The
compilation of these numbers appears to have contemplated
both the provision of new houses for the poorly housed
and the stabilization of the home building industry at a
level of production that would be nearly a third higher
than the number ever produced in any decade in history,
notwithstanding that the effects of World War II and of
the forces affecting housing demand that it and its after-
math released were very rapidly diminishing and little or
nothing in the economy of the nation had appeared to replace them or substitute for them.

Not much attention had been given prior to 1973 to
the efficiencies and deficiencies of the programs established during the whole period from the early 1930s
through the depression, the war, and the sequel to both.
On the whole, the Congress has only been urged to strength-
en the hands of those administering these programs, principally by appropriating larger and larger sums to be spent
on these, or on programs that merely supplemented them and
embodied all their imperfections as well as their merits.*

Especially missed is comment and analysis of the relationships between the administration of these programs
and the course of costs of construction and housing
prices and rents. The purpose of the Congress in adopting
these proposals seems to have been to assure construction
of the number of units prescribed, regardless of the
amount of subsidization necessary to achieve it.

The drive of the officials of the HHFA and HUD has
been in the direction of increasing the volume of production, principally by assuring producers of a market for
their product at their prices, by making prospective purchasers of members of low- and lower-middle-income groups,
even though these could be enabled to purchase at these

----

*The scandals that broke out over the operations con-
ducted under Title VI of the National Housing Act (admin-
istered by the FHA) in the early 1950s and Section 235 in
the fall of 1971 sparked immediate and "thorough" investigations by the appropriate committees of the Congress, and
especially by the FHA and HUD, followed by assurances that
these were probably due entirely to the malfeasance of
field officials, in conspiracy with local "outsiders,"
both of government or individual purchasers or builders,
or both. Little has been said or done about the inherent
weaknesses of these programs that make such irregulari-
ties likely in their conduct.

prices only if they could secure credit for a larger and larger portion--and finally for the whole--of the builders' asking prices.

As these suggestions were adopted by the Congress and enacted into law, not only was encouragement given to the rise in costs and prices, but the necessity for subsidization was extended to a larger and larger portion of the households seeking homes.[6]

Thus the program of government subsidies has tended to enhance rather than to diminish the force of the ratchet process of increasing costs and prices and to throw upon the government a larger and larger burden of subsidies necessitated by its moving further and further into the market.

TABLE 8.3

Number of Standard Metropolitan Statistical Areas Having Minimum and Maximum Percentage of Growth in Population by Migration, 1960-70, by Population Size Groups, with the Numbers (in thousands) and Rate of Gain or Loss

Population Size Group	Number in Group	Losing		Gaining	
		Number	Highest Rate	Number	Highest Rate
Over 2 million	12	5	-7.8[a]	7	20.2[f]
1 to 2 million	21	3	-6.4[b]	18	78.3[g]
500,000 to 1 million	32	6	-7.5[c]	26	76.7[h]
250,000 to 500,000	60	23	-13.1[d]	37	85.4[i]
Under 250,000	118	57	-32.7[e]	61	49.3[j]
Total	243	94			

[a]Pittsburgh   [f]Washington, D.C.

[b]Buffalo   [g]Anaheim and so forth

[c]Jersey City   [h]Fort Lauderdale

[d]Corpus Christi   [i]Las Vegas

[e]Brownsville and so [j]Colorado Springs
   forth, Texas

Source: U.S. Bureau of the Census, Census of Population and Housing, 1970, "General Demographic Trends for Metropolitan Areas, 1960 to 1970," Final Report PHC (2)-1, p. 47, Table II.

It might not be inappropriate here to call attention to the fact that in contemplation of and following the passage of the Act of 1968, mandating the most colossal volume of construction ever contemplated and at least implying that funds would be made available to enable subsidization of the portion of that volume that was necessary to secure its realization, from 1967 to 1971--in four years--the Boeckh index of cost of residential construction rose by nearly 33 percent, and the average sale price of new houses purchased with the assistance of FHA mortgage insurance rose by 28 percent, from $18,611 in 1967 to $23,835 in 1971 (see Tables 8.2 and 8.3).

As previously suggested, the tendency for costs and prices to absorb the amounts made available to prospective purchasers or renters has plagued government programs since the first, introducing the Federal government into direct participation in the construction and rental markets, was launched in 1934.[7] Close examination of these tendencies indicates that promises of extending the loan-value ratio of the mortgage and extending its term so as to make home purchase "possible for lower income prospective purchasers" may bring greater profits and wages to builders, building suppliers, and building labor rather than assisting lower and lower-income households to compete in the market. Similarly, maximum costs, rents, and prices set by law or by regulation very promptly have become minima as well as maxima.

CAPITAL VERSUS OCCUPANCY COSTS

The concentration of the Federal housing authorities on construction of new units has ignored another dichotomy that is important to the understanding of housing markets: the distinction between capital costs involved in the development of new facilities and the costs of occupancy involved in their use. The roles of these two types of costs in housing markets are quite different, as is the way in which they find expression in prices and rents.

All the costs incurred in assembling a site, planning the construction of housing units and the infrastructure essential to urban living, assembling labor and materials for construction, interest charges for borrowed funds needed in this preliminary phase and during the process of building, lawyers' and accountants' fees--all the expenditures involved in the prosecution and consummation of one of the most complex transactions in modern society

constitute the capital cost of building or development of
housing facilities. And, most important to the understanding of the behavior of these markets, all these costs
have to be incurred or their payment contracted for before
construction actually begins. As progress is made toward
the finished product, payments toward meeting these costs
must be made, for the most part in cash or its equivalent.

But the costs of development are incurred but once;
once incurred or contracted to be incurred, they are sunk;
they can be recovered only by the sale of the rights held
in the premises that they were instrumental in producing.
The extent to which they may be recovered with possible
profit or loss, depends not upon their magnitude when they
were incurred. It depends solely upon what the owner of
the premises can get in the market in which he offers the
rights to their occupancy and possession for sale in per-
petuity or for rent over a limited period of time.

If the development is one of single-family houses
for sale to prospective owner-occupants, what the developer can get depends upon his finding purchasers who are
able and willing to pay the price he asks, which, of
course, includes both his capital costs and his profit
(and frequently in the postwar period, a larger profit
than he anticipated when he made his commitments). But
he knows before he makes his commitments, in most cases,
that the ease and readiness with which he will find such
purchasers will be in direct proportion to the ratio of
the amount of a mortgage loan he can secure for a purchaser to his asking price and in inverse proportion to
the amount of monthly payment required to pay the interest and amortize the mortgage over its term. He therefore usually has an agreement with a mortgage lender in
which the terms he is able to promise the purchaser have
been agreed upon. And the amount is usually enough to
refund to the developer all his costs of development, and
a considerable part if not all of his profits.

The "speculative," "operative," or "merchant" builder,
therefore, is always urging that the terms of mortgages
eligible for insurance by the FHA or VA (which set the
standards for the whole industry) should include those
with the highest possible ratio of loan to the prices he
hopes to realize.

So great has become the dependence of large-scale
home builders on selling to purchasers on easy terms that
many of them will not make commitments to develop and
build until arrangements are made through the VA and the
FHA (or a private mortgage insurer) for acceptance of the
mortgage for insurance and guarantee in the amount agreed

upon, subject only to the builder's producing an eligible borrower, acceptable to these agencies as well as to the mortgage lender.

And much of the volume of home construction for sale is not actually initiated until after the sale is made. This delay of starts has been growing since the huge volume of construction engendered by the government campaign of 1970 began to come on the market.

In March 1970, according to the reports of the Bureau of the Census, 19 percent of the sales of new homes were made before construction began, and 34 percent while the homes were under construction. In March 1974, only 12 percent were sold before construction began, and 39 percent while construction was under way. The percentage of all sales made before construction was completed fell from 71 percent in June 1971 to 51 percent in March 1974 (see Table 8.4).

That is, in March 1974 on 12 percent of the "starts for sale" the builder took no risk of finding a buyer; and on 39 percent, the risk had disappeared before the structure was completed. It appears that the "speculative builder" no longer "speculates" on getting his price for the finished product; he wants the "down payment" in hand for at least half of his products before they are completed.[8]

It has been argued by both the builders and some of the officers of the FHA that the extension of terms, including increasing the maximum amount of the mortgage as well as a maximum loan-value ratio required for eligibility, has benefited the many American families which would not otherwise have been able to purchase new homes on terms that correspond to "their ability to pay." Less has been said about how these changes have enabled the speculative homebuilder to dispose of his product at prices that have risen more rapidly during the whole postwar period than have those of any other type of economic goods of the price behavior of which close track is kept.[9]

The market for the completed house is much wider as the amount of the down payment is reduced. Some prospective purchasers do not have very much ready cash or readily convertible assets by the sale of which they can acquire ready cash; and those that do have may not want to part with either large amounts of cash they have on hand or liquid assets they have carefully accumulated over time. And some may not want to make a large down payment because they feel it would constitute putting "too many of their eggs in one basket."

TABLE 8.4

Percentage of New One-Family Homes Sold While Under
Construction or Before Started at the End of the
Month of Sale, March, June, and September, 1970-73
(seasonally adjusted)

| Year and | Stage of Construction* | | |
Month	Both	Under Construction	Not Started
1970			
March	53	34	19
June	56	38	29
September	57	38	29
1971			
March	60	44	16
June	71	50	21
September	65	46	19
1972			
March	65	49	16
June	67	50	17
September	63	44	19
1973			
March	60	42	18
June	57	41	16
September	68	52	16
1974			
March	51	39	12

*At the end of the month of sale.

Source: U.S. Bureau of the Census, Construction Reports, "New One-family Homes Sold and For Sale," C-25-72-10, and C-25-74-4.

Whatever the motives, the smaller the down payment
and the periodic payment, the easier and more certain the
sale (regardless, almost, of the length of time over which
the periodic payment is promised).

So the Bureau of the Census reports that of the
572,000 new homes sold during 1972 (for which sale price
was reported) 91,000 (16 percent) were bought with no
down payment; an additional 128,000 (22 percent) paid
from 0.1 to 4.9 percent down; that is, 38 percent of
those who used mortgage money used more than 95 percent

of the amount needed to pay for their house; and over 50 percent paid down less than 10 percent of the price they agreed to pay.[10]

Further, it must be noticed, this "speculative" volume produced by the builder appears to be the most erratic item in the whole array of new units produced. For example, when total starts dropped from 1965 to 1966 by 314,000 units, "privately owned single-family" starts accounted for a decline of 185,000, of which 151,000 were for sale. That is, 82 percent of the drop in single-family starts was accounted for by decline in the number started that were for sale. Single-family producers were "limiting their exposure" and threatening the gross national product.

It seems reasonable to presume that so long as the speculative builder can offer his house for sale at a price and on such terms that the purchaser's cash outlay does not exceed, over a period of two or three years, say, what he would have to pay for rent if he chose to rent, he will have little trouble or expense in selling his product.

Nor will he have much incentive to save costs and to pass those savings on to his purchasers.

Nor would it seem unreasonable to assume that when his costs and consequent prices rise to the point where he may be unable to promise such generous financing terms to his prospective purchaser, he might threaten to reduce his prospective volume of construction. And if no measures are taken to enable him to proceed as usual, he might actually reduce his volume of production--and thus jeopardize the prospect of a rising gross national product.[11]

In fact, this may be a brief statement of what has happened several times in the postwar period! And may partially account for the large increase in residential building costs and prices! (see Tables 1.2 and 8.4).

Two observations need to be made about the results of these changes in mortgage terms that have characterized the period from 1929 to the present, with rapid acceleration of the rate of their adoption and use in housing production markets during the postwar period: (1) it seems clear that the capital required for development of additions to the inventory of housing units is no longer provided by the builder or developer or their purchasers but principally by the mortgage lender. In other words, the "speculation" involved in planning and developing housing facilities has become less and less a function

performed by the "speculative builder" and more and more
one that has to be borne by the speculative builder's
financing agent; and he, in turn, leans more and more
heavily on his mortgage insurers and his buyers (see Table
8.5); (2) the periodic out-of-pocket expenditures of the
purchaser of the new home, including the down payment,
have been reduced to and maintained at a level that just
about covers operating costs and the debt service on a
mortgage loan that "bails out" the builder, with his
profits, and that are not any greater, and in many cases
less, than the periodic rent that the purchaser would
have to pay for occupancy of housing facilities that com-
pare in amenities and comforts (but not in size) with
those he acquires by his purchase.

In making his purchase, therefore, the purchaser of
the new house is placed in the position in which he can
profit in a rising market by selling the thin equity he
slowly acquires by making his slender down payment and
his small periodic mortgage payments. For to this thin
equity he can add the increment in price that has occurred
during the period of occupancy, minus, of course, his
costs of selling.

On the other hand, he stands to lose little from a
declining market; for he can go into default in payment
of his debt service, vacate the house when he has to, and
invite the mortgagee to foreclose; or, give him a "deed
in lieu of foreclosure" to save the troubles accompanying
foreclosure. Upon the lender, then, falls the risk of
losing a part of the capital investment which he extended
to the builder; and he, in turn, can pass this risk on to
another purchaser, if he can find one. Or if the mortgage
was insured by the FHA or the VA (or a private insurer) he
can look to the insurer to "bail out" at least a part of
his capital.*

This is exactly what has been happening over the last
ten years. While most of the first and second (or third)
purchasers of the newly built home have been able to find
a purchaser of their equity when they had to sell, at a

----

*From 1952 to 1956, the percentage of properties ac-
quired by FHA-insured mortgagees by foreclosure and then
transferred by deed to the FHA rose from 57 to 87. During the second half of the decade of the 1950s, it ranged
from 80 to 87; and during the 1960s from 89 to 97. In
1970, it stood at 92, and in 1971 at 91.

TABLE 8.5

The Number of Starts of New Housing Units Reported in the
Fourth Annual Report, Achieved During the Years 1969-72;
Targeted Number Scheduled in the Second Annual Report
for the Years 1973-78[a], with Number and Percentage
of Total Unsubsidized and Subsidized
(not including mobile homes or rehabs)

Year	Total	Not Subsidized		Subsidized	
		Number	Percent	Number	Percent
Grand total	23,664.2	19,080.6	80.6	4,883.6	20.3
Achieved:					
Total	6,957.2	5,638.6	81.0	1,318.6	18.9
1969	1,600.2	1,436.9	89.7	163.2	10.3
1970	1,359.4	1,062.9	78.1	296.5	21.8
1971	1,797.6	1,358.8	75.5	438.8	24.4
1972	2,200.0	1,780.0 (5,639)	80.9	420.2	19.1
Targeted:					
Total	16,707	13,442	79.0	3,565[b]	20.9
1973	2,250	1,955[c]	76.6	595	23.3
1974	2,800	2,200	78.5	600	21.4
1975	2,950	2,355	79.8	595	20.1
1976	2,925	2,330	79.6	595	20.3
1977	2,925	2,330	79.6	595	20.3
1978	2,857	2,272	79.5	585	20.4

[a]This schedule was not revised in either the Third or
Fourth Annual Reports.

[b]From Second Annual Report, p. 26.

[c]From Second Annual Report, p. 5.

Source: Calculated from tables in First, Second,
Third, and Fourth Annual Reports on National Housing
Goals.

price that covered the costs of selling and a profit on their equity, from 1962 through 1972 the FHA and the VA have bailed out lenders on about 576,000 insured mortgages--an average of 57,000 a year. The cost to the FHA in connection with its more than 400,000 cases in which it has acquired title will be, judging from past experience, between $500 and $575 million. Or, to put it another way, some $2,500 to $3,300 of the capital invested by mortgage lenders on the security of these mortgages will have been written off at the expense of the Mutual Mortgage Insurance Fund.

And at the end of the year 1972, the FHA had on hand nearly 61,000 homes, owned "projects" that contained more than 22,000 rental units, and held defaulted mortgage notes covering 71,000 units--thus easily retaining its position as the nation's, and probably the world's, largest seller of homes and residential landlord.[12]

The practices followed in the development and management of rental projects follow much the same kind of pattern. The developer, who may be a builder, a real estate broker, or anyone who wants to undertake planning and building a project, cannot be expected to, and as a rule does not, make binding commitments to proceed to develop housing facilities until he is convinced that by so doing he will be able to realize a minimum profit from his venture--a profit that is in proportion to the risks and return he might receive from placing his time and other resources in other kinds of activities. But once he has made the decision to invest in a housing venture and has made binding commitments to landowners, contractors, architects, and the dozen or more other parties concerned, he is bound to complete the project, or "go broke."

And whether he goes broke is determined, not by what it costs to complete the project, but by what he can get in the market as net rents or lump sum price for his interest in the premises he has created.

It is important to note, again, that the capital costs of development are sunk by the developer in the process of development. Forever afterward, the value of ownership in a rented development is independent of the amount of development costs and dependent upon what the owner and prospective bidders for his interest believe they can net in future rents or by subsequent resale of that interest.

> Current income, if any, flows from the
> sale of rights to use and occupy space
> within the structures. Rents paid for

these rights reflect market conditions
prevailing at the time the leases are
signed. In that sense, they bear no
necessarily fixed relation to the amount
of capital invested in developing the
structures or in acquiring ownership in-
terests in them. Nor are they necessarily related to the burden of current operating expenditures, or to the amount
of debt service payments--fixed at an
earlier time--which must be met currently if owners are to maintain their
equity positions unimpaired.[13]

During 1970, the Bureau of Census reports, over 12 percent of the apartments constructed were sold to prospective occupants as cooperative or condominium owner-
occupants. This is another method by which the developer
can get his equity and profit out in cash in a short
period of time, and at a higher rate of profit.

In opening the premises for occupancy, therefore,
the developer of multifamily units will set up a schedule
of rents that will give him, or at least appear to give
him, maximum net returns. The schedule necessary to
cover operating costs (and in most cases also the debt
service) and a minimum net return to equity constitutes
a floor below which he will not go unless and until persistent vacancies make it appear that this is his only
recourse in a falling market.

In many cases, he has acquired tenants for the majority of the units at rents that may be inflated by concessions granted to the first occupants. These make the
costs of occupancy to these tenants during the term of
these leases acceptable, and they make the volume of
gross collectible rents appear higher than those actually
collectible from these tenants may be after the terms
covered by the first leases have expired. In New York in
1962 such a large number of apartment units were being
completed to "get in under the wire" before more restric-
tive provisions were incorporated into the zoning regulations that in order to preserve what seemed like a high
level of gross rents, concessions became quite commonly
advertised. Some of these were so liberal as to offer a
"free trip around the world for two people" provided they
would sign a two- or three-year lease. The practice became so prevalent and so deceptive in Chicago in the late
1920s that the legislature of the State of Illinois, at
the insistence of title companies and mortgage lenders,

111

passed an act which provided that on any lease of real estate premises in connection with which concessions were granted, the words "Concession Granted" should be printed in "letters one inch high."

That the practice was not confined to Chicago, nor to the present century, appears evident from the following quotation:

> It is the custom in some parts of the city (New York) for the speculative builder to fill up his building with tenants upon its completion, giving them often three months' rent free, and in many cases signing bogus leases purely for the purpose of impressing the purchaser or investor of the property with the idea of the large rentals to be secured from it.[14]

A report issued jointly by the Bureau of the Census and the Department of Housing and Urban Development indicated that in apartment structures containing 127,323 units, completed in the third quarter of the year 1973, 75 percent of the units had been rented in three months. Of 142,262 units completed during the same quarter of 1972, 69 percent were rented in three months; and 86 percent of 87,303 completed in that quarter of 1971 were rented in the same period. Of those completed during that quarter of 1970, 77 percent were rented in three months; and of the 792,051 units completed in the fourth quarter of 1969, 82 percent were rented in three months. That is, this percentage of completed units in apartment houses rented in three months dropped from 82 percent in 1969 to 77 in 1970, but rose to 73 percent in 1973--a drop of 18 percent from the point it had reached in 1969.[15]

The lump sum that the developer frequently realizes from sale of his interest in the completed project represents the capitalization of the net rent that the purchaser thinks he can realize from operating the project and from the resale of his interest after the operating period he contemplates has ended. Disappointment may come to the developer or to any one of his successors in interest from (1) a higher rate of vacancy than he contemplated when he made his commitment; (2) a lower rent schedule he may be forced to adopt or perpetuate by the imposition of some form of rent control or in the effort to reduce vacancies; or (3) higher costs of operation than he had contemplated.

Conversely, his profit will be expanded by (1) a lower rate of vacancy than he expected to have to carry; (2) ability to secure higher rents than he expected without incurring unexpected vacancies; or (3) lower costs of operation than were anticipated. Obviously, the thinner his equity, that is, the smaller the amount of his own capital invested permanently in the equity, the greater the effect of these unanticipated changes upon his total profits as well as on his rate of profit or loss. If, after receiving the proceeds of the permanent mortgage, he has no actual cash or its equivalent invested, his profit may be infinity, or his loss zero. Or, in recent years, he may be able to profit by taking an accounting loss by charging the highest permitted rate of depreciation on the buildings as an operating cost, and thus deducting from federally taxable income his bookkeeping loss, saving taxes that would be payable on income from other sources. In many cases, it is the privilege of taking "accelerated depreciation" covering the cost of the buildings on federal income tax reports that induces investors to participate in development of large rental projects.

> Accelerated depreciation and interest cost deductions loom importantly in tax loss calculations because of the leverage effects the investor can take advantage of. Real estate properties [presumably the development or purchase of the equity in real estate properties is meant] are usually financed by a mortgage loan covering about two-thirds to 90 percent of the project cost, with the owner's equity providing the remaining 10 to 33 percent [the spread would be more realistic if it read "the remaining 0 to 10 percent"]. Yet the owner is permitted to depreciate the entire cost of the building, including the portion financed by the loan. And, a larger loan increases interest cost deductions, while decreasing the amount of equity funds that have to be furnished by the investor.[16]

It must be added that local real estate taxes, paid by the owners of rental properties, are also a deductible expense before calculating the net income subject to Federal income taxes. Yet, in another part of the Fourth

Annual Report it is said that "The tax incentives (deductibility of home mortgage interest and local real estate taxes) help homeowners of all income classes, with the greatest benefits accruing to homeowners in the higher income brackets."[17] Presumably Federal housing officials consider that the homeowner-occupant as an investor is entitled to less tax consideration than is the investor in rental facilities.

It is also worthwhile to notice here that, although the developer may reduce his contribution in the form of cash or its equivalent as far as possible so as to achieve maximum "leverage," his activities as a promoter or entrepreneur may justify his participation in any profits that may accrue to the participants in the enterprise. The value of his services is frequently depreciated.[18]

When the costs of operation, including local real estate taxes, of privately owned multifamily projects, rise more rapidly than the owner or his managing agent can raise rents, the increase in costs acts to reduce the value of the owner's equity. And if his equity is thin, that is, if a large portion of his gross rent collections is absorbed by the costs of operation and his debt service, he comes, after some time, to try to find a "sucker" who believes he can increase the net returns by raising the rents or by "milking the property," or he proceeds to milk it himself. By "milking the property" the trade means skimping on repairs and maintenance and neglecting the payment of taxes.

By resort to these "tricks," in many instances, the owner of the equity can recover a considerable part of his actual capital investment, if any, before depreciation, deterioration, and the tax collector catch up with him. The sophisticated investor will not long keep pouring money not received from operation into the unavoidable expenditures of operating. To do so, he holds, is too much like pouring sand into a rat hole: there is little chance that any of it will ever be recovered.

But when both maintenance and the payment of taxes are neglected, it is not long until rapid deterioration sets in and accumulates at a constantly accelerating rate. Sooner or later, individual ownership is abandoned, and the whole neighborhood becomes derelict and a community liability. Then all the units in the area become substandard in the sense that their occupants do not enjoy a house that is "decent, in a suitable environment."

It is thus clear that one of the facts of life about rental housing, regardless of who is the owner, is that someone must pay as a minimum rent enough to cover the costs of occupancy, including the upkeep and maintenance of the unit and the structure in which it is located and the local taxes levied against it. And so long as title remains in private hands, there must be something left over after these costs of operation have been met. Further, the amount left over, not the costs of development, determines the value of the equity.

Two other things need to be said about the costs of operation: (1) these vary greatly by type of residential structure; and (2) the level at which they are kept depends very much upon the ability and skill of management. The tasks of management are so complex and involve so many kinds of business and social contacts and transactions that the inexperienced or untrained manager may make many avoidable mistakes in either business or personal relations. These may involve excessive costs in the form of abnormal rate of turnover of occupancy, discontent and rapid turnover of service personnel and tenants, above-lowest-market prices paid for equipment and supplies, and inefficient use of both supplies and personnel.

It takes experience and training to learn many of the costsaving tricks that can be used in balancing expenditures and results in the management of the high-rise, multifamily structure.

NOTES

1. For a forceful and accurate statement of this radical feature of housing markets, see Harold Wolman, Politics of Federal Housing (New York: Dodd, Mead, 1971), p. 22. Cf. also David M. Blank and Louis Winnick, "The Structure of the Housing Market," The Quarterly Journal of Economics 67 (May 1951): 181.

Another distinguished housing economist has put it this way: "Generally, a housing demand estimate, based entirely upon national aggregates, is virtually meaningless and can lead to grave . . . miscalculations. . . .

"Use of national figures on population or household growth does not account for the effect of international migration upon housing demand." Lawrence N. Bloomberg, "Housing Demand Analysis in Developing Countries," Proceedings, Social Statistics Section, American Statistical Association (1966): 161.

2. See, for example, Peter C. Goldmark, "The Need for a New Rural Society," in Michigan Business Review 26

(May 1974) 3:5, for a brief summary of research being done
at the University of Michigan and financed by HUD on the
planning and development of a semiurban, semirural community in which the new means and methods of communication
will probably reduce greatly the dependence upon the automobile for commuting to work in both manufacturing and
administrative locations.

3. According to the Bureau of the Census, nearly 20
percent of the population one year old and older "had been
living at a different address one year earlier" when the
population survey was made in March 1971, and the percentage of movers had been close to this figure for most of
the years 1948 to 1971. U.S. Bureau of the Census, Current Population Reports, Series P-20, No. 235, "Mobility
of the Population of the United States: March 1970 to
March 1971" (Washington, D.C.: Government Printing Office,
1972).

4. U.S. Bureau of the Census, Census of Population
and Housing, 1970, "General Demographic Trends for Metropolitan Areas, 1960 to 1970," Final Report PHC (2)-1
(Washington, D.C.: Government Printing Office, 1971).

5. Some of the basic economic forces were mentioned
and assigned to four categories by officers of the FHA in
Hearings before the Subcommittee on Housing of the Senate
Banking and Currency Committee of the 84th Congress in
1964 (p. 237):

> 1. Areas subject to sharp, localized
> economic fluctuations . . . have been
> noteworthy in Detroit and other automobile
> manufacturing centers in Michigan, and in
> Wichita, Fort Worth, and Philadelphia.
> 2. Areas affected by reduction in
> defense and military employment or deacti-
> vation of military bases. . . .
> 3. Interruptions of growth rate in
> expanding areas . . . areas experiencing
> very rapid growth, when the growth rate
> slowed down, even for a short period
> . . . Orlando, St. Petersburg, and Miami,
> Florida, are outstanding examples.
> Houston, Texas, also reflects this situ-
> ation.
> 4. Areas of chronic unemployment.
> . . . Coal mining in West Virginia and
> Pennsylvania are examples of this, as are
> certain textile manufacturing areas in
> New England.

6. As one of the previously highly placed officials
of HUD pointed out in a memorandum prepared while he was
the senior research housing specialist in Congressional
Research of the Library of Congress, with respect to the
subsidization of mortgage interest rates, the extension
of subsidies to higher and higher income groups "tends to
be self-defeating"; as it increases the number of potential recipients of subsidy, it reduces, more than pro
rata, the number of unassisted market participants and
swells disproportionately the volume of federal funds
needed to meet the demands of both bodies of recipients.
But as qualified buyers enter the market for the limited
supply of new houses, builders are not slow to recognize
that the increase in the number of bidders will support
an increase in their prices--and they cannot be blamed for
asking for them. And as soon as they demonstrate that
they can get them, two things happen: (1) the suppliers
of building materials and building labor demand a share of
the "windfall"; and (2) the builder and the lender do not
find it difficult to convince the mortgagees' appraisers
that current prices and costs justify higher appraisals.
So the "circle of economic relationships" is closed, and
the new level of prices and costs becomes fixed in the
market for both the new and existing units in the inventory. See Henry B. Schecter, "The Residential Mortgage
Financing Problem," a paper submitted to the Subcommittee
on Housing of the Banking and Currency Committee of the
House, printed for the use of the Committee, 92nd Congress,
1st Session (Washington, D.C.: Government Printing Office, 1971), p. 44.
7. Under the provisions of legislation and regulations governing FHA operations since World War II, both
the loan-value ratio and the term of years for mortgages
eligible for insurance by the FHA have been liberalized
several times: in the early 1950s the maximum term was
20 (or, in limited cases, 25) years; in 1961, it was extended to 35 years for new construction. In 1953, the
maximum loan-value ratio was 95 percent; in 1957, it was
increased to 97 percent. The VA guarantee, during the
whole postwar period, could cover 100 percent of the purchase price, except for a few years in the early 1950s.
    During the four years 1957-60 the average cost of
acquisition of new homes purchased with the assistance of
FHA increased by $398. After the increase of permitted
term of the mortgage to 35 years in 1961, this cost increased at the rate of $345 a year for the next four
years, a total of $1,380. After 1965, the average annual
increase jumped for the next four years to $695, and for

117

the following seven years by more than $1,000 a year, to
$24,367 in 1971. And the new Bureau of the Census' new
home price index jumped from 1960 to the third quarter of
1971 at an average annual rate more than three times that
of the increase from 1963 to 1965 (see Table 8.4).

It may be noticed, further, that notwithstanding the
rapidly rising prices of new homes from 1968 to 1971, in
the latter year the Federal Home Loan Bank Board authorized, under certain specified conditions, insured savings
and loan associations to make 95-percent loans. Previously their limit was 90 percent of appraised value.

For a recent and disturbing illustration of these
tendencies in operation, see the story entitled "The Well-
to-Do Get Subsidized Housing," in the Sunday New York
Times for August 20, 1972. In this article, it is stated
that "rents in Mitchell-Lama subsidized new buildings will
soon exceed $100 per room per month," and these units will
be available to households with incomes "as high as
$50,000." Mr. Walsh, head of New York City's Housing and
Development Administration, is quoted as saying that while
the original guidelines have changed sharply, the housing
program has not evolved into an outright rent subsidy for
upper-income families. "But if you're asking if we're
trying to keep the $40,000-to-$50,000-a-year family in
the city, the answer is yes" (Section 8, p. 1).

8. U.S. Bureau of the Census, Construction Reports,
"New One-Family Homes Sold and For Sale," c25-74-4.

9. For a detailed description of the influence of
one of the organizations of the building industry in
securing passage and favorable administration of the
legislation that may have contributed to this end, see
"The Homebuilders' Lobby," by William Lilley III, re-
printed in Housing Urban America, eds. Jon Pynoos, Robert
Schafer, and Chester W. Hartment (Chicago: Aldine, 1973),
from National Journal (February 27, 1971).

10. U.S. Bureau of the Census, Construction Reports,
Series C-25: "Characteristics of New One-Family Homes,
1972," p. 99.

11. Several years ago Louis Winnick pointed out:
"A housing policy aimed only at the lower- and middle-
income classes, on the theory that the higher-income
groups can fend for themselves, overlooks two things:
first, the mere financial ability of the well-to-do to
spend more on housing does not ensure that they will
spend more. The well-to-do are already satisfactorily
housed. They must be induced to upgrade." Foote, Abu-
Lughbod, Foley, and Winnick, Housing Choices and Housing
Constraints (New York: McGraw-Hill, 1960), p. 19.

And one cannot help adding that the residential
building and closely associated industries have never
taken any lead in inducing "the well-to-do" to "upgrade"
their housing instead of their automobiles--or (one can
hardly refrain from adding) their cosmetics. Instead of
competing with other groups for the consumers' dollars,
the residential building industry and its associates have
turned to the Federal government for assurance of their
market at their desired prices and in the volume they can
convince the officials is necessary to maintain a continuous increase in its contribution to the gross national
product.

One of the perverse features of house-building costs
is their tendency to increase (over the whole country) as
the volume of production increases, contrary to the behavior of costs incurred in usual manufacturing operation.
Even in the individual operating unit, Maisel found, increases in volume might account for only 5 to 15 percent
in savings. And in an industry whose product is salable
in only a very limited local market, it is not necessary
for the large-scale builder to give his buyers the price
advantage that this possible saving in costs makes possible. It may be used to increase profits instead.
Sherman J. Maisel, Homebuilding in Transition (Berkeley
and Los Angeles: University of California Press, 1953),
p. 202.

12. HUD Statistical Yearbook, 1972, pp. 194, 195.
In the Fourth Annual Report on National Housing Goals reference was made (p. 30) to the fact that foreclosure
rates "on such mortgages" (insured by the FHA in connection with the administration of the Housing Act of 1968
that ". . . changed the 'economic soundness' prerequisite
for mortgage insurance 'in older declining urban areas'
and substituted an 'acceptable risk' for a property in
such an area . . . have been steadily rising."

But nothing is said further about the rates of foreclosure; instead, it is indicated that "The inventory of
HUD properties represents the net difference between units
acquired following such foreclosure and the units sold in
order to recoup as much as possible of insurance losses.
One measure of the magnitude of the problem, therefore,
would be the size and composition of HUD-owned units at a
point in time. . . . Although the trend of acquisition
continues to rise, the inventory as of March 1 [1972] was
43,084 homes, less than 1 percent of total insurance in
force, and less than in 1964 . . ." (when the number was
51,971).

But in discussing even the inventory as a signal of FHA (or HUD) distress, no mention is made of the number of cases or units in connection with which, in accordance with the contract of insurance, the holder of the insured mortgage, on which delinquencies have accrued, may assign the mortgage to the Secretary and file his claim.

So, even by the criterion of inventory of units and assigned mortgages on hand, HUD experience must have been reflecting some serious distress in the housing mortgage markets of the country as early as December 1972.

13. Robert Moore Fisher, "Mortgage Delinquencies and Foreclosures as Symptoms of General Market Behavior," 1964 Conference on Operations, Audit and Control of the National Association of Mutual Savings Banks, Philadelphia, February 18, 1964.

14. Robert W. DeForest and Lawrence Veiller, The Tenement House Problem (New York: The Macmillan Company, 1903), vol. I, p. 374.

15. U.S. Bureau of the Census, Current Housing Reports, "Market Absorption of Apartments: Fourth Quarter, 1972" and ". . . Fourth Quarter, 1973," H-130-72-4; H-130-73-4.

16. Fourth Annual Report on Housing Goals (Washington, D.C., June 29, 1972), p. 51.

17. Ibid., p. 42.

18. Louis Winnick, Rental Housing: Opportunities for Private Investment (New York: McGraw-Hill, 1958), pp. 87ff.

9

**PROGRESS TOWARD
THE "GOAL"**

The "National Housing Goal" established by the Congress in 1949 was the "realization as soon as feasible of a decent home and a suitable environment for every American family." In several official pronouncements concerning this goal, the expression "for every American family" became transformed into "for every American," and finally in the President's Second Annual Report on progress toward the completion of 26 million new and rehabilitated units by 1978, coverage of the expression was further expanded into "the proposition that everyone should have the opportunity to live within a reasonable distance of his job and daily activities."

In the Housing Act of 1968, the Congress boldly declared that this goal could be "substantially achieved" by the building or rehabilitation of this exact number of units by the end of the year 1978. No one in authority has challenged the validity of the Congressional assertion that the addition of 20 million new units to the inventory and the renovation of 6 million of those standing in 1968 would "substantially achieve" the goal of "a decent home and a suitable environment" for all.

Instead, after the Republicans came into office in 1969, the new Secretary of Housing and Urban Development stated: "I accept the 26 million housing goal set by Congress . . . as a reasonable statement of the minimum need--in fact I think we need more than 26 million."[1] In the Second Annual Report on National Housing Goals, the following statement appears:

The original estimate of the 10-year housing need was prepared two years ago under the

previous administration. In order to make
a thorough examination of developments since
that time and completely reevaluate the ways
in which the housing goal can and should be
met, a new interagency housing task force
was established this past summer. The task
force is chaired by a member of the Council
of Economic Advisers and has representatives
from the Departments of Housing and Urban
Development, Agriculture, Labor, Treasury,
and Commerce, the Federal Home Loan Bank
Board, the Federal Reserve Board, and the
Bureau of the Budget. It now reports to the
Cabinet Committee on Construction. This
[the third] Annual Report of National Housing Goals reflects the preliminary findings
of the task force.[2]

Apparently the task force did not challenge the total numbers standing in the Act of 1968 nor their realization as
a means of realizing the original Congressional goal, but
were content to rearrange the quotas for the future years
of the decade and introduce mobile homes as a source of
supply.

So these numbers, enshrined in the statute books,
have become sacrosanct--their achievement made obligatory
on the Federal officials upon whose shoulders rests the
responsibility for administration and enforcement of the
laws.

And even after these highest officials had been suc-
ceeded by Republicans, they accepted the goal as both
reasonable and minimal. The only question that seems to
have bothered them was whether the economy as organized
could meet the challenge and actually produce somewhat
over a third more units than it had in the fantastic
1950s.

So the new Secretary of the Department of Housing and
Urban Development announced, after he had been in office
nearly two years:

From a housing production standpoint . . .
one principal significance is the clear
evidence that we have it within our ability
to produce the housing units called for by
the National Housing Goal established by
Congress in 1968. . . . At the time this
Administration took office there was

122

widespread skepticism . . . as to the Nation's ability to achieve this goal. There
should no longer be any doubt on this score.
     This means that this year of 1971 is a
year in which a significant stride has been
taken toward a reduction of our Nation's
critical shortage of adequate housing. . . .
With the President's new economic program of
curbing inflation, the prospects for an even
greater level of housing starts in 1972 are
exceptionally good.[3]

Events confirmed this optimism; later in the year
1971 it was pointed out that: "The annual figures . . .
obscure the most significant development that occurred in
the housing sector during the past year: the downtrend
in production that began in early 1969 was brought to an
end in the spring of 1970, and there then followed a very
sharp rebound that brought production at the end of 1970
to the highest rate in 20 years."[4]

Scant reference was made in this Third Report to the
changes that had been made in the Second Annual Report
from the schedule of "production" set down by the former
administration in the First Report. The most significant
of these changes were (1) the total number of unsubsidized
starts scheduled had been reduced from 20.2 million to 16
million, or from 77.1 percent of the total "target" to
61.5 percent; (2) in the first schedule, no mention was
made of mobile homes, but in the second, for the whole of
the decade, mobile homes were scheduled to provide 4 million units, 15.4 percent of the total target; (3) while
the total number of units to be provided by subsidization
was kept the same (6 million), the number provided or to
be provided during the fiscal years 1969 and 1970 was reduced by 725,000, and the number to be provided without
subsidy was reduced by 420,000 for the first two years
and by 2,310,000 or a total of 2,730,000 for the first
four years of the decade.

By this manipulation of numbers, the whole quota for
production without subsidy was reduced by 420,000 for the
first two years, and that with subsidy by 217,000--a total
reduction of 637,000 units. But by the inclusion of
817,000 mobile homes as a part of production the total
schedule was increased by 176,000, and despite the "less
than expected production of mobile homes, rehabilitations
of substandard units under subsidized programs, and on-
site starts of new units without benefit of assistance

from subsidy programs . . . the total production goal of
1.85 million units was almost achieved."

The schedule or quota as established in the Second
Annual Report was not changed in the Third and Fourth Annual Reports, but in each of these, there was much ado
about achieving or surpassing the "goals" set forth in
that schedule. In the Fourth Annual Report, it was indicated that

Total housing production in calendar 1971--
including starts, mobile home shipments, and
subsidized rehabilitations--amounted to 2.6
million units. The total housing starts
broke the previous record established in
1950. [See previous pages for an account of
this record.]
        Progress toward reaching the national
housing goal set in the 1968 Housing Act . . .
is running well ahead of the production path
outlined in the Second Annual Report on the
Housing Goal. The fiscal year 1971 housing
production total was 2,273,500 units, which
exceeded the FY 1971 goal by 233,500 units.
The FY 1972 goal of 2,330,000 units . . . is
expected to be exceeded by about 500,000
units. On a cumulative basis, housing production for the first four years is estimated
to be 8 percent ahead of the goal path, as
revised in 1970.[5]

In the exultation over this heroic performance, no
mention is made of the fact that the shipment of mobile
homes accounted for more than 1.7 million of the new units
produced, and that 16 percent of the achievement resulted
from the subsidization of starts or rehabilitations--that
is, 3 million of the targeted production had come from
these two sources.

Less than 80 percent of total production during these
four years consisted of newly built units. The 650,000
units scheduled to be produced with the aid of subsidy
during fiscal year 1972 constituted 31.8 percent of the
total new construction target. The number of "subsidized
starts" scheduled for the first four years of the decade
had been increased from 475 to 1,435,000--from 5.7 percent
to 17 percent of the total production scheduled (see
Table 9.1).

In summary, by this change in the number and type of
units to be produced, the Department was able to report

TABLE 9.1

Projections of Volume of Subsidized, Unsubsidized, Rehabilitated, and Mobile Units to be Produced Each Year in the Decade 1968-78 in the First and Second Annual Reports of the President on National Housing Goals

Year	Total	Not Subsidized		Subsidized Starts and Rehabilitated		Mobile Homes		Subsidized and Rehabilitated	
		Number	Percent of Total	Number	Percent of Total	Number	Percent of Total	Number	Percent of Total
First Annual Report:									
Grand total	26,200	20,200	77.1	6,000	22.9	0	15.4	2,000	7.6
1969	1,675	1,450	86.5	225	13.4	0	18.1	50	2.9
1970	2,000	1,500	75.1	500	25.0	0	24.3	100	5.0
1971	2,225	1,600	71.9	625	28.1	0	23.2	150	6.5
1972	2,375	1,750	73.6	625	26.4	0	19.3	175	7.3
1973	2,575	1,950	75.7	625	24.3	--	16.9	--	--
1974	2,650	2,000	75.5	650	24.6	0	13.6	175	8.4
1975	2,950	2,300	77.9	650	22.1	0	12.9	250	8.4
1976	3,200	2,500	78.4	700	21.8	0	11.7	275	8.6
1977	3,250	2,550	78.4	700	21.6	0	11.4	325	10.0
1978	3,300	2,600	78.7	700	21.3	0	10.4	325	12.5
Second Annual Report:									
Grand total	26,000	16,000	61.5	6,000	23.0	4,000	15.4	5,000	19.2
1969	2,001*	1,440*	71.9	198*	9.8	363*	18.1	155*	7.7
1970	1,850	1,090	58.9	310	16.7	450	24.3	260	14.0
1971	2,040	1,060	51.9	505	24.7	475	23.2	445	21.8
1972	2,330	1,230	52.7	650	27.8	450	19.3	575	24.6
1973	2,650	1,505	56.8	695	26.2	450	16.9	595	22.4
1974	2,930	1,800	61.4	730	24.9	400	13.6	600	20.4
1975	3,085	1,955	63.4	730	23.6	400	12.9	595	19.2
1976	3,060	1,980	64.7	730	23.8	360	11.7	595	19.4
1977	3,060	1,980	64.7	730	23.8	350	11.4	595	19.4
1978	2,994	1,960	65.4	722	24.1	312	10.4	585	19.5

*Achieved.

Sources: Calculated from First Annual Report on National Housing Goals, pp. 8, 14; Second, p. 23.

at the end of the first four years of the decade that the
target had been met, even exceeded; that this record of
production could be characterized as the nation's "largest
housing production surge in history," and that "the outlook for 1972 is bright. New starts and subsidized rehabilitations could again reach around 2.1 million units.
. . . Subsidized housing could push total production as
high as 2.8 million units."

Thus, through the first four years of the "crisis"
decade, the attention and the principal efforts of the administration were kept focused on the production of new
houses, and especially those for moderate- and low-income
households.

It was not until the Third Annual Report on National
Housing Goals appeared that the Federal housing authorities called attention to a possible role for the standing
stock in providing "a decent home" and a "suitable environment." In that report, a whole section is devoted to
"Maintenance of Housing Stock." Here it was said that

> As the continuing inflation of housing costs
> has priced more and more American families
> out of the housing market [apparently mean-
> ing new housing markets], there has been in-
> creasing pressure for the Federal Government
> to move in to fill the cost/income gap by ex-
> panding subsidy programs at enormous cost of
> Federal budget funds. This was most dramat-
> ically evident in the pressure in the Congress
> last year to extend the housing subsidies now
> available for low- and moderate-income fami-
> lies into a new program that would subsidize
> middle-income families as well.
>
> In calendar year 1968, the Federal gov-
> ernment subsidized about 10 percent of all
> new housing produced; last year, the figure
> was up to almost 25 percent and it is sched-
> uled to remain in this range this year and
> next. It is estimated that subsidized
> housing units started or projected for the
> 3 fiscal years 1970-72 have already obli-
> gated the Federal government to subsidy
> payments of perhaps $30 billion over the
> next 30 to 40 years.

After they had been two years in office, devoted to
strenuous promotion of increase in the volume of new

construction, housing officials seem to have realized that the adoption and prosecution of a program of building new houses for all income groups, and especially for those whose incomes were not large enough to enable them to pay rapidly accelerating prices for these products of the building industry, involved governmental expenditures and commitments that might tax the resources even of the not-too-affluent United States.

In recognition of this trend, the Secretary of HUD testified before the Appropriations Committee of the House, that "The tab for subsidized housing is going up, and as housing costs [he probably meant house building costs] soar, the number of families [he probably meant households] needing subsidies is increasing alarmingly."[6]

In the Third Annual Report, on page 24, the same concern about costs appears: "At present, the maximum subsidy paid through a combination of programs is about $2,400 per unit per year."

These expressions of concern with subsidy costs reappeared in the Fourth Annual Report, in an even more "alarming" form. Here it was written:

> Whenever the Federal Government pays the
> difference between the cost of large numbers
> of new units built to high standards and
> what a lower income family can afford, major
> expenditures are involved. . . . It can be
> projected . . . that the Federal Government
> is already committed to about $12 billion
> in future subsidies for these programs
> [Sections 235 and 236] alone, based on the
> number of units approved through FY 1972,
> although the maximum payments legally per-
> missible could reach as high as $36 billion.[7]

That is, the Federal government may be committed to three times what it is admittedly obliged to pay in the future on these two programs.

When this forbidding outlook is related to the statement in the Third Annual Report, page 23, that "By the end of Fiscal Year 1972, 2 million or more families probably will be receiving housing subsidy under one or another of the many Federal programs. The amount of such subsidies range as high as $2,400 per family per year," it is easy to see why Federal officials began to worry about the costs of subsidization programs that placed emphasis "almost exclusively on new construction." For, when the

5,907,900 units scheduled in the Second Annual Report for "production" with subsidy is multiplied by $2,400 per unit, the annual outlay by the Federal government comes to more than $14 billion. And many, probably most, of these outlays would be committed for a term of years reaching 40, and probably averaging 35. Placing an estimated $14 billion fixed charge for 35 or 40 years on the Federal budget that is currently running a deficit of up to $36 billion should cause some pause on the part of responsible governmental officials.

The Third Annual Report suggested that one of the features of national housing policy and programs that might be contributing to the magnitude and rapidly rising governmental expenditures involved is "the emphasis placed on linking the Federal subsidy almost exclusively to newly constructed housing units." This emphasis was defended on the ground of "the desire to use Federal subsidies to provide as much stimulus as possible to housing production." "But the result is," the Report went on to point out, "that eligible families in many communities are moving into brand new homes on which they make relatively modest payments while other families in similar . . . circumstances are left struggling to meet their monthly payments on older homes purchased without subsidy."

A third aspect of governmental housing programs that is mentioned in this report is "the relationship between national housing policy and the environment--both physical and social."

It was promised in this report that during the coming year (FY 1972; Calendar, 1971) existing Federal housing policy and programs would be subjected to close scrutiny and study would be focused on "cost, equity, and environment"--"so that necessary reforms in basic policy can be identified, developed, and implemented as quickly as possible."

The Fourth Annual Report took up the discussion by stating first that "The fact that the nation has the productive capacity to reach the 26 million goal is no longer a serious question. . . . The real question is whether a strategy which focuses narrowly on housing production alone will bring the nation to the qualitative goal of 'a decent home and a suitable environment for every American family.'"

It then proposed to continue the discussions initiated in the Third Report under the headings: "housing programs, housing strategies, and housing as a component of the community environment--both social and physical" (page 28).

But under these headings little was said about how existing "programs, strategies" and the environmental effects of existing programs were developing and whether these strategies should be changed, supplemented, or abolished. It was admitted that

> the two new categorical housing subsidy programs enacted in 1968 dominate the discussions. . . . Two new interest subsidy programs, one for subsidized home ownership (section 235), and one for subsidized rental (section 236), were enacted and Congress has since provided the budget authority and appropriations necessary for volume production.
>
> HUD has experienced operating problems in both the newer interest-subsidy programs and the high-risk inner city programs. Continuous surveillance over program operations has uncovered many instances of loose program processing, shoddy construction, excessive profits, and consumer victimization.[8]

This confession was made before the extent of the fraudulent practices that had been prevalent in a number of large metropolitan offices was recognized. It would be pointless to emphasize here either their magnitude or their near universality.

> A second broad area of discussion in the last year involves the question of balance in the Federal government's housing strategy, particularly the balance between programs which subsidize the production of new housing, and programs which subsidize the people in their efforts to find decent housing in the existing housing supply. The major subsidized housing programs tend to favor the production of new housing, and thus seek to accomplish the dual objectives of increasing the supply of housing, and of helping eligible families to pay for new housing they could not otherwise afford. This combination of objectives has two consequences which are causing concern. The first is that the programs involve a relatively expensive method of adding new units

129

to the housing stock. The second is that
relatively few families in relation to the
eligible population actually receive the
direct, special income assistance provided
by these programs, and furthermore, the
families which benefit most are usually not
among the nation's most needy.[9]

In view of these criticisms, the HUD budget for the
fiscal year 1973 "envisions a substantial increase in the
use of existing housing, particularly in the public housing program, which is the primary federal program for
assisting low income families." And it appeared that, at
least, the Federal authorities were beginning to pay some
attention to the use of the standing stock.
In fact, a four-page appendix is devoted to a discussion of the standing stock. The major conclusions announced here are: (1) an increase of 10.3 million units
in the interval between the Census of 1960 and that of
1970 was noted; (2) the degree of "overcrowding" is noted
to have decreased during the same period; (3) the number
of "substandard" units was suspected of having been reduced from 10.6 million in 1960 to 5.2 million in 1970;
(4) an "increase of almost 30 percent in 8 years in expenditures by private owners for maintenance, repairs, and
major replacements" was mentioned, and (5)

the average (median) age of the housing
stock declined from 28 years in 1950 to 27
years in 1960, and it is estimated to have
been at 26 years in 1970. . . . Under
normal use, and with proper maintenance, a
residential structure can last several
generations, limited only by changes in
taste and the costs of modernization. However, no matter how well maintained an individual housing unit or residential structure may be, the surrounding environment
ultimately becomes decisive on the continued
usefulness and quality of the housing services provided by the structure.[10]

In each of the Annual Reports, there is a discussion
and a "projection of the residential mortgage market needs
and prospects during the coming year, including an estimate of the requirements with respect to the availability,
need, and flow of mortgage funds . . . during such year,

together with such recommendations as may be deemed appropriate for encouraging the availability of such funds,"
as is required by the Act of 1968.[11]

It is strange that in none of these reports is mention
made of the current rate of delinquencies and foreclosures
of residential mortgages, and their influence on "the
availability" and "flow" of "such funds." Yet, as has
been pointed out, the rate of both these phenomena rose in
the late 1920s and in each post-World-War-II period when-
ever the rate of construction reached and passed the peak
--in 1926 and in 1955, 1958, 1965, 1968, and 1973. Yet
there is no reason to believe that private markets will
respond to increasing home mortgage delinquencies, followed by rising rates of foreclosures, in the future differently from the way they have responded in the past.
If they do, even the reduced quotas assigned to unsubsidized starts may not be "achieved," and the burden on the
Federal budget--current and contingent--further increased
to make up the shortage.

And, in fact, these consequences may already have
begun to appear. The appearance of increased delinquencies and foreclosures would not be expected until after
newly constructed units are completed and come on the
market. Since 1968, the Bureau of the Census's reports
on "Completions" indicate that these follow starts with a
lag varying from two to four months. The nation's "largest housing production surge in history" reached its first
production peak (five months moving average, centered on
three) in June, 1971; "completions," in October.

The percentage of FHA-insured mortgages "seriously
delinquent" rose from 1.69 at the end of the year 1970 to
1.92 in 1971, for those insured under Section 203; from
4.27 to 5.65 for those insured under Section 201(d)(2);
and from 1.96 to 4.26 percent for those insured under
Section 235(1).[12] The total under all these sections was,
as indicated before, at the rate of 2.31 in December,
1971 and 2.75 for 1972--the highest rate on record.

Delinquencies reported by the Mortgage Bankers Association rose from 2.96 percent at the end of the first
quarter, 1970, to 3.21 for 1971; and from 3.10 at the end
of the third quarter, 1970, to 3.59 in 1971; and to 4.01
at the end of the first quarter, 1974.

The rate of delinquencies on all nonfarm mortgages
held by reporting life insurance companies rose from .65
percent at the end of 1970 to 1.31 percent at the end of
1972; and to 1.57 in 1973.

The foreclosure rates have followed suit; the rate
of foreclosure on all property, reported by the Federal

Home Loan Bank Board, rose from 3.44 for the year 1970, to 4.11 for the year 1972; and for all mortgages held by insured savings and loan associations, from .186 for the year 1970 to .199 for 1972.

During the year 1972 FHA acquired 50,256 homes, 74 percent more than during the year 1970; and at the end of 1973 had 75,269 homes "on hand," and 233 "projects" containing 23,235 housing units. Altogether, then, it was owner or landlord of 98,504 units. In addition, it is reported that as of December 1973 the Secretary held mortgages that had been assigned to him on account of delinquencies, covering 1,282 "projects" containing 127,394 housing units.[13] The Federal government was then involved in ownership and operation of some 226,000 housing units and was coendorser of mortgage bonds issued by local public housing authorities, or has committed to them to become coendorser for some $16 billion dollars which have been or are to be used to "develop" "low-cost housing" for close to 1.7 million households in cities and villages scattered throughout the United States. The Federal government has thus strengthened its position as largest landlord, operator, and financier of housing in the country, and probably in the world.

It may be, further, that the large number of starts that were recorded during 1971 and 1972 and the succeeding volume of completions are beginning to affect the vacancy ratios reported in the surveys of the Bureau of the Census. According to the report for the first quarter of 1974, the rental vacancy rate for the whole United States stood at 6.2 percent, the highest rate reported since 1968; and the "homeowner" rate at 1.2 percent, 0.2 percent higher than in the first quarter of each year since 1969.

But in the South, where the greatest surge of construction has been seen, the rental rate was reported at 7.9 percent, and the homeowner rate at 1.4 percent.

It may also be mentioned that the inventory of unsold new homes has been increasing since this volume of new construction reached such unprecedented dimensions. According to the report of the Bureau of the Census on sales of new houses dated February 1974, the total number of new homes available for sale at the end of February 1974 was 459,000; at the end of February 1973, 420,000--an increase during the year of nearly 10 percent. The number sold during February 1974 was estimated at 42,000 units, down from 58,000 during December 1973--a decrease of 28 percent. Builders can not be expected to maintain a large volume of starts when the overhang of unsold new homes is as large as these numbers suggest.[14]

If these trends should continue throughout the calendar year 1974, privately owned unsubsidized starts may
follow the course they have persistently followed since
World War II, in the face of these trends. If they do,
it would not be surprising to find that, even if there
were a huge inflow of funds into mortgage-lending institutions, some hesitancy of mortgage officers of these institutions to place their funds into residential mortgages
might develop. If it does so, there will probably follow
a great deal of agitation for further intervention by the
Federal government and its agencies and those over which
it has major control in the market to achieve the sacrosanct goal and enable the residential construction industry to "make its appropriate contribution to the nation's
gross national product."

Then, as was said in the Third Annual Report, the
only way in which the production "goal" of new units could
be achieved would be by increasing the volume to be purchased with the aid of subsidization, even beyond that set
out in the Second Annual Report. The same set of circumstances would dominate the markets for new houses that
prevailed when it was written in the Third Annual Report:

> In many instances, production under one of
> the various subsidized housing programs was
> the only way a builder could be relatively
> assured of finding a buyer who could afford
> the monthly payments associated with a newly
> produced housing unit and also finding mort-
> gage money to finance the construction and
> purchase of the units. Thus many builders
> who had long avoided involvement with Fed-
> eral subsidized programs shifted to where
> the action was in order to remain in busi-
> ness during the overall production decline.[15]

It could not be more clearly stated that so long as
the Federal government seeks adequate housing for every
American only in newly built units, it will be obliged to
"assure" the builder "of finding a buyer who [can] afford
the monthly payments." There is no other available method
by which this assurance can be given and of assuring that
the industry will make its maximum contribution to the
gross national product, as has been indicated above (see
page 24).

NOTES

1. In an address by the Secretary to the Mortgage
Bankers Association of America, as reported in HUD *News*,
"for immediate release, October 21, 1969."

2. Ibid., p. 21.

3. HUD *Newsletter*, vol. 2, no. 48, December 27, 1971.

4. "Third Annual Report on National Housing Goals,
Message from The President of the United States" (Washington, D.C.: Government Printing Office, 1971), p. 6.

5. *Fourth Annual Report on National Housing Goals*
(Washington, D.C., June 29, 1972), pp. 1, 2.

6. Quoted from HUD *Newsletter* of May 1, 1971.

7. *Fourth Annual Report on National Housing Goals*,
p. 29. The total number of units on which HUD had made
commitments under these two programs through fiscal year
1972 was approximately 463,000 units. If these numbers
are correct, the commitment is approximately $20,000 per
unit and the contingent liability three and one-half times
that, or approximately $78,000 per unit. At $5\frac{1}{2}$ percent,
the annual contribution, if commitments are for 35 years,
would be a minimum of $1,690 per unit and the maximum,
$5,070. The minimum would pay the debt service on a 35-
year, $5\frac{1}{2}$ per cent completely amortized mortgage of about
$26,000; and the maximum, of about $78,000.

8. *Fourth Annual Report on National Housing Goals*,
p. 30.

9. Ibid., p. 31.

10. Ibid., p. 39.

11. Title XVI, Section 1602, P.L. 90-448, August 1,
1968.

12. See Table 6.2.

13. HUD *Statistical Handbook*, 1972, pp. 129, 156, and
194; HUD Memo report as of December 31, 1973.

14. U.S. Bureau of the Census and HUD, *New One-Family
Houses Sold and For Construction Reports*, C-74-2, February
1974.

15. *Third Annual Report on National Housing Goals*,
p. 7.

10

NEEDED CHANGES IN FEDERAL HOUSING PROGRAMS

More than five years of experience with the Act of 1968, with the heavy pressures it produced on administrators for "achievement" of the quota of 20 million new homes and 6 million subsidized rehabilitations, have brought widespread recognition--even among those engaged in and responsible for operations under the Act--of its inappropriateness.

They have also brought into focus the failures and extravagances that have plagued the administration of many of the other Congressional mandates with respect to housing of the poor that have been issued over the past three decades: even the mistakes in emphasis and method of operation that were inherent in the United States Housing Act of 1937 that put the Federal government directly into active intervention in the thousands of local housing markets scattered from Maine to Hawaii, and from Key West to Nome. Evidence of disillusionment is abundant and finds its most authoritative expression in the resignation of the recent Secretary of Housing and Urban Development, and in some of his public statements.

The way out leads first through a complete overhauling and revision of the relevant legislation and a reorientation of the whole process of Federal government intervention in local housing markets.

Over the three postwar decades, programs and appropriations approved by the Congress have either patched up current programs or supplied an increasingly large stream of public funds said to be needed to make these programs effective. As one Senator put it:

> I've been on the banking committee of the
> House and Senate now for nine years. . . .
> Every year we've gone through exactly the

same experience--we open our hearings on
the authorization for housing and urban
development or the appropriations. The
experts from HUD and from the rest of the
country come to us; they spend days--
often weeks--telling us why what they
said last year had been proven wrong, why
the programs they had proposed last year
had not worked, and how the only response
we could make would be to double the number of programs and the appropriations.
The pattern just seems to roll over on
itself every year.[1]

The criticisms that appear most valid of the programs that culminated in the Act of 1968 may be summarized as follows:*
1. Each separate program, beginning with the United
States Housing Act of 1937, has been proposed, considered,
and passed by the Congress upon assurance of proponents
that it would alleviate if not cure the deplorable conditions in which the poor urban families are living. In
urging passage of the Act of 1937, the proponents asserted
that the intended beneficiaries were members of the lowest income groups. Gradually--and sometimes not so grad-
ually--the benefits were proposed to be extended upward,
until in the Act of 1968, they included the low- and
moderate-income families.

With each extension of the income limits of eligible
beneficiaries, the funds needed to implement the programs
suggested grew in geometric progression as the number of
recipients and the proportion of total number of qualify-
ing families to be benefited increased. As a consequence,
although appropriations, commitments, and disbursements
bulged at accelerating rates, the goals presented to the
Congress receded at an equally accelerating pace after
each recommended measure was adopted.

---

*These comments are similar in many respects to those
included in a report prepared by the author at the request
of the Administrator of HHFA in 1960, entitled "A Study of
Housing Policies and Programs." Many are also similar to
some of the proposals contained in "Report and Recommendations of Three Study Panels of the Subcommittee on Housing . . ." of the Committee on Banking and Currency of the
House of Representatives 92nd Congress, First Session,
dated June 1971, specific references to which are omitted
here.

In presenting the budget of HUD for the fiscal year 1973, the Secretary testified that "payments for assisted housing" for the fiscal year 1971 amounted to $851,600,000, and covered 393,396 starts. For the fiscal year 1973, he was asking for $1,878 million and estimated that by the end of that year, the number of starts receiving subsidy would have risen to 564,000. Over the three-year span, the increase in the amount of funds disbursed or requested was more than $1,026 million dollars, 120 percent; while the number of subsidized starts increased or was expected to increase by only 50 percent (see Table 10.1).

TABLE 10.1

Increase in Numbers of Housing Units on Which Subsidy
Payments Were Made or Were Committed, or on Which
Such Payments Were Anticipated in Budget Requests
for the Fiscal Years, 1971, 1972, and 1973

Year or Years	Amount for Subsidies ($000,000)	Numbers of Assisted Starts
1971 (Actual)	851.6	393,396
1972 (Estimated)	1,373.8	500,800
1973 (Requested)	1,878.0	564,000
Increase:		
1971-72:		
Amount or number	522.2	107,404
Percent	61.3	20.7
1972 to 1973:		
Amount or number	504.2	63,200
Percent	36.7	12.2
1971 to 1973:		
Amount or number	1,026.4	170,604
Percent	120.5	50.5

Source: HUD Newsletter, February 7, 1972, Vol. 3, no. 6.

While the number of households that would be considered eligible for subsidy cannot be calculated with mathematical exactness, the Secretary of HUD stated in the Third Annual Report on National Housing Goals that:

the number of American families who are
receiving large Federal subsidy payments
to assist them in buying or renting a
place to live is increasing rapidly. By
the end of the fiscal year 1972, 2 million more families probably will be receiving housing subsidy under one or
another of the many Federal programs. . . .

Under present law, as many as 25 million American households--40 percent of
the total population--are eligible for the
major subsidy programs. If all eligible
families were subsidized, the cost would
be astronomical.

2. Legislation enacted since the 1930s, especially
in the postwar period, and the programs that it established, represent an ad hoc, fragmented approach to many
aspects of the processes of building housing facilities,
of buying and selling them and of managing them.

These processes and practices are complicated; they
employ persons with a great variety of skills and abilities; probably most importantly of all, they require the
investment of large amounts of capital, most of which is
customarily borrowed by those who are active in creating,
buying, and selling or managing them. Most of the legislation enacted during the postwar period has been ad-
dressed to only one restricted aspect of these processes
and practices; and the effects of its enactment and administration on other aspects have been ignored. As a result, the programs have not been adapted to the entire
market process but to only a fragment of it.

In some instances they have supplemented the actions
and programs of the private sector; but probably in more
they have supplanted them. Instead of recognizing markets
as wholes, they have further fragmentized them. In many
cases, they have had contradictory effects, especially
when the purpose or objective sought by the program authorized was not clearly stated.

Thus, although the programs authorized and conducted
have been numerous, their total impact upon bad housing
conditions has been much less than it might have been if
these fragmented efforts had been combined into a single
consistent drive toward a well defined objective.[2]

As Secretary Romney has expressed it: "The problems
have generated and multiplied so rapidly that it's more
than governments can do to keep up. Our band-aid response

has not been getting to the source of the pain. We have passed laws and instituted programs on a piecemeal basis that result in a fragmentation of effort."[3]

3. The parallel between the increases in the "costs" (prices or rents) of new housing units and the increases in the amount and percentage of needed funds that could be obtained on mortgages by lengthening their terms and reducing the loan-value ratio raises the radical question of whether the disbursements made to assist purchasers (and renters) have not benefited others more than those whom they were intended to relieve.

The largest groups to whom it is sometimes suggested some of the benefits may have flowed are the builders, building labor, the suppliers of building materials, and real estate brokers and speculators.

It has been thought by some observers that this tendency for subsidies to be diluted in the process of reaching those whom they are intended to help may be at least partly attributable to the provision in most of the programs that assigns the subsidy to a housing unit rather than to people who may require financial help in order to acquire the right of occupancy and use. Making the subsidy payable on account of the new unit is intended to increase the volume of production; for every subsidy paid or promised to be paid, the argument goes, assures one more unit added to the inventory, while payments made to a household may merely aid it in moving into an existing unit.

Of course, this is true. But the recipient who uses the subsidy to secure occupancy of an existing unit may be one who vacates a substandard unit and thereby improves his housing conditions; and in many cases, as already indicated, he may do so at a lower cost than if he occupied a new unit for which he can pay the builder only if he has a subsidy; and what is saved in subsidy may be used to assist another household to improve its housing conditions.

But, of course, the subsidy paid to enable two households to upgrade their housing conditions by moving into existing units does not enable the builder to contribute to the gross national product--nor to his own profits. So these two objectives of some of the housing programs conflict; and in existing programs and their administration, the one that enables the builder to contribute to the gross national product and increase his profits, pay more wages to building labor, and buy more building materials from the manufacturers and distributors has thus far been favored.[4]

139

4. Responsibility for detailed direction and supervision of the transactions contemplated by these programs has been concentrated in one Federal government agency in Washington. As a result of this concentration of authority and power, notwithstanding the building up of a huge bureaucracy, the millions of transactions involved have been slowed up--entangled in a web of red tape. Compliance with the rules and regulations that constitute this web not only slows up consummation of these transactions; it also leaves widespread temptations to fraud and imposition upon those who are presumed to be the system's beneficiaries.

As is indicated elsewhere, the law governing the transfer of rights in real estate is the creature of the state in which the real estate lies; and there is a considerable variation in the details incorporated in these laws. And real estate and housing markets are uniquely local in scope. This means that there are 50 states in which the provisions of the law with which the details of a transaction must comply may vary; and within each of these jurisdictions there are a number of important markets which are loosely connected, if at all. The organization sufficiently large and with necessary training and supervision to participate in transactions in the hundreds of thousands of local markets throughout the nation cannot be kept flexible, dependable, and prompt in responding to demands made upon it for decision and action.

During its five years of existence, Secretary Romney reported in a press release (HUD No. 7--443) dated June 22, 1970 that

> Responding to a Presidential directive, the U.S. Department of Housing and Urban Development has taken steps to scrape off the administrative barnacles which have caused a drag on the delivery of HUD's programs and services to the public.
>
> HUD Secretary Romney announced that six key programs have been revamped to step up their efficiency and delivery time. . . .
>
> The Secretary said he was particularly pleased that a substantial number of man-years would be recaptured and used now to give greater service to communities within existing budget ceilings. . . .
>
> During the year [his first in office] we have restructured the Department along

functional lines, established the frame-
work for the new 10-regional field pattern, and developed a new field structure
which includes area offices located in
population centers, offering easy access
to the full scope of HUD services.

In view of the necessity for making contact with
millions of individual citizens and hundreds of thousands
of institutions, it is no wonder that "administrative
barnacles" would have accumulated to the point of creating
a "drag on the delivery of HUD's programs and services to
the public."
As of June 1973, the Department was "expected to
have" on its payroll 15,836 "full time employees," according to its Newsletter, dated February 12, 1973 (vol. 4,
no. 7).
One can only wonder whether a "restructuring" of such
a huge bureaucracy, involved in participation in hundreds
of thousands of individual transactions in local markets
scattered so widely, and necessarily conforming to different laws in 50-odd jurisdictions (including those in Guam,
Puerto Rico, and the Virgin Islands), can be made to operate effectively and promptly in even a majority of these
cases.
This weakness in the structure of federal programs
can be eliminated by relieving the Federal government
from participation in and supervision of the details of
individual transactions in the hundreds of thousands of
local market transactions and placing that responsibility
on local public agencies. These can be made familiar
with and trained in the use of the instruments and processes adapted to the locality.
The development of state housing and development
authorities is a movement in this direction. In one or
two states, these agencies have been set up and have operated efficiently, promptly, and effectively. Before
they and such other public agencies as local public housing authorities or, as cited in the 1949 Act, "local public agencies," can become established as major factors in
the solution of local housing problems, they must be
staffed with personnel recruited and trained in all the
major phases of real estate market behavior, such as
negotiation, law, building, management, and financing.
And before they can become effective in dealing with
those who need help most with their housing problems,
they must be trained in many of the aspects of social

141

work. In short, their staffs must become experienced and
sympathetic social workers as well as able and well-
rounded real estate brokers, developers, and managers.
The assumption that public agencies of this scope and with
these abilities could be created in 48 states spontaneous-
ly after the passage of the act in 1937, when such agencies existed in only one state, New York, was either naive
or intentionally misleading. Even after more than 30
years of experience, few of these local housing authorities are equipped to perform all the functions involved in
one of the most complex operations in the urbanized society, and the state agencies referred to above, equipped
to supervise local authorities, exist in only two or three
states. This may be only a political weakness in our national housing programs and policies, but it is no less,
therefore, an essential structural weakness that will have
to be strengthened before federal programs result in
alleviating the housing problems of the poor.

An admirable course of training for prospective managers of housing occupied by low-income tenants has been
conducted in England for a century by the Octavia Hill
Association. A branch in Philadelphia has also operated
gracefully for several decades and in 1973, according to
its 77th Annual Report, collected over $250,000 in rent
from tenants of 269 dwelling units. Median rent collected
was $76 a month.

The functions of the responsible federal agencies
could be centered on the development of policies and programs that were benefited by experience as it developed.
The federal establishment would also be constantly engaged
in the analysis of operating experience and in the preparation of plans and instructions, including the huge task
of training personnel in the intricate processes of improving the housekeeping--and living--standards, even the
economic and financial management abilities of those who
have least to spend and should therefore spend what they
have as effectively as possible.

Local public agencies would receive detailed instruc-
tion in how to set up a project, prepare a budget, and
manage a housing program for the poor; the Federal government would make a lump sum grant of the funds found to be
justified, and subject the local agency to post audit,
not to the meaningless submission to the Federal authorities of all the details of a transaction for approval before it could be consummated.

In short, the authority, the ability to make final decisions, and the power that accompanies these, must be

decentralized in more than promise. This process may not appeal to Federal authorities, including the Congress, but it is essential to effective and efficient programs of housing relief for the poor who live in our slums and blighted areas.*

5. Failure to adjust programs to changing conditions is another condition that needs remedy.

> Effective action programs must be adjusted to changing social and economic conditions. For real estate and housing markets, the most important social and economic conditions include employment and unemployment, especially in the building trades; the level and distribution of income in the community; the rate of utilization of the standing stock of housing facilities; the prevailing level, direction and magnitude of change in building costs, prices, and rents; and changes in the number and in the demographic characteristics of the local population.[5]

Direct Federal governmental intervention in local housing markets was initiated in the early 1930s; since that time vast changes have come in every one of these major aspects of social and economic conditions. At that time, all types of construction were at an almost complete standstill; incomes had skidded in every community in the country, and for many households had completely disappeared. Vacancies in every kind of real estate facilities were at an all-time high; the rate of utilization at an all-time low. Costs of building were steady or declining, and prices and rents had fallen by significant amounts and were at the lowest levels seen since 1919.

One of the major purposes of all of the legislation thrusting the Federal government directly into housing markets was to bring some relief to the moribund construction industry and other industries closely related to it; to relieve some of the unemployment in the building trades and in economic activities such as the manufacture and distribution of building materials and of the varied types of furniture and furnishings that are closely tied to building.

---

*The subcommittee of the Banking and Currency Committee of the House recommends "block grants" but leaves final decision on payments to HUD.

Opposition to the programs initiated during the 1930s
arose largely from fear that adding to the inventory of
facilities of all sorts would deepen the distress of owners and managers of the standing stock (including homeowners), a large part of which was idle. The costs of
building had fallen so far that newly constructed units
could be offered for sale or rent at prices and rents below those required to cover the operating costs and debt
service on existing facilities. It was thought by many
observers of housing markets in many places that further
construction could only deepen the distress of these owners and managers.

But by the time the Housing and Redevelopment Act of
1949 was enacted, and the resplendent goal of "a decent
home and a suitable environment for every American family"
announced by the Congress, conditions in every one of the
items mentioned above as critical in housing markets had
been reversed; employment in the building and allied trades
and in those economic activities closely related to them
was at a peak; incomes throughout the society had been re-
stored and greatly increased; savings in liquid form had
accumulated; vacancies had almost disappeared, and a large
portion of the married couples in all large urban communities were unable to find a separate housing unit; the
house-building industry was one of the most prosperous
and busiest in the whole economy.

And these conditions were not fundamentally changed
in most urban communities during the whole decade of the
1950s. There were some reverses in some communities during the 1960s.

But during both these decades, the type and purpose
of the programs of intervention by the Federal government
urged upon and adopted by the Congress followed closely
the pattern established in the 1930s.

Instead of suggesting adaptations of the existing
programs to these changed conditions, proponents of further government intervention, for the most part, plead
for extending the limiting provisions of existing programs
to include more and more types and a larger and larger
portion of existing and prospective households, and for
increasing the appropriations necessary to cover both the
increases in number of eligible households and in the
amount of subsidy needed to cover the higher prices and
rents they would have to pay for more elaborate and expensive units, as Senator Brock complained.

The principal adaptation that this comment suggests
is that of shifting the emphasis of governmentally supported programs to a much greater use of the standing

144

stock and less to the subsidization of the building process. There may be localities that are still in need of acceptable housing units and in which there are some households that cannot afford to pay for the right of occupancy of standard units at prevailing prices or rents for units that become available in the usual course of market events; but the deficit of standard units is no longer widespread even in our most rapidly growing metropolitan areas.*

If this kind of shift of government housing policy results in some decline in the aggregate number of new

---

*In all the discussion of the inability of the lower-income groups to afford a standard housing unit at going prices and rents, there has been little attention paid to the items that enter into and determine the amount of these costs, except as they apply to costs of occupancy of newly built units and include such capital items as interest and amortization of mortgage indebtedness (which in some cases covers the entire expenditure necessary to develop a project). Such scanty statistics as have been assembled, however, suggest that the recurring costs of operation—such as heating, lighting, janitorial services, security provision, and real estate taxes vary greatly by type of structure, and are highest in high-rise, elevator-equipped structures; and that in these, operating costs increase more than proportionately as the size of structure increases. All these costs (with the possible exception of real estate taxes) are lowest in the structure in which the spaces that are common and must be maintained by management are minimal. But the public housing programs have paid little attention to this distinction and discussion has focused almost entirely upon capital costs; that is, the costs of amortization and interest on borrowed capital. And many of the projects built by local public housing authorities since 1937 have been unable to collect from tenants enough rent to cover these operating costs alone. It was this observation that prompted the author to suggest in his 1960 report to the HHFA Administrator that local public housing authorities should "begin to build up an inventory of graded public housing facilities" so that "the principal criterion of capital investment on the part of the local authority [could become] . . . the largest number of eligible households that could be assisted with the given amount of resources and within the requirements of a balanced inventory."

units built in a year with an accompanying decline in the contribution that housing construction makes to the gross national product, let more of the resources used up in building new houses be more effectively employed in the maintenance and improvement of individual units and the whole environment surrounding the existing inventory.

But, it may be contended, the standing stock has become too far deteriorated and would cost too much to justify putting these resources into that endeavor.

There can be no definitive reply to this contention. It can only be pointed out that 20 or 30 years ago, when the shift of emphasis was called for by the changes that had come to the economy, this deterioration had not gone so far that it could not have been stopped, or at least very greatly slowed up, at what would have been then a smaller investment of resources than would be required now.

And, much more importantly, if some such shift in emphasis is not soon adopted, tens of thousands--no, hundreds of thousands--of the existing stock in or near the hearts of our major urban centers will over the next decade or two join the dying and decaying units that now haunt many blighted or slum areas. While there may be units and even blocks that are so far gone that the only appropriate prescription is that embodied in the Act of 1949--bulldoze the whole area--there still remain hundreds of thousands of blocks in which nearly all the units can still be saved--provided action is taken to save them instead of hastening their decay by building new units in farther outlying areas and making them available to the occupants of those now declining--regardless of the cost to the public in both dollars and the social resource the existing inventory represents.

6. Probably the most fundamental weakness of Federal housing programs is attributable to the underlying assumption upon which they are based; that the problems of those who live in the slums and blighted areas can be solved and the evils that pervade them can be driven out by the abolition of "substandard" housing units and the provision of new units made available to these families and households.*

----

*The same assumption seems to underlie the proposal of substituting "housing allowances" to these poorly housed poor. The extension of cash for payment of housing costs would undoubtedly help some households to obtain possession and use of better housing than they now

146

But recognition of the complexity of these problems and of the inadequacy of any single type of solution has become widespread. There is developing a far-reaching and pervasive search for the basic causes of these deplorable conditions and for a simultaneous and coordinated program directed toward removal or destruction of these causes.

And certainly among the most important, if not the most important, of the causes being recognized is failure of municipal authorities to provide the full complement of public services to these areas. As soon as garbage and trash begin to accumulate in the streets and on the sidewalks and life and property protection becomes neglected, school authorities begin subtly to discriminate against the local school, loiterers (including some who peddle illegal wares) appear on the street corners, some landlord or landlords discontinue checking on the character and reputation of one or more of their prospective tenants, refuse to maintain their structures in good condition--and the whole area soon becomes "blighted" or "slums."

And while the absurd contention that "people make the slums" has long since been abandoned by any but the most ignorant, it has become widely recognized and acknowledged at the same time that there are no slums where there are no people.

It is a common observation among apple growers that "one bad apple in a barrel will cause the whole barrelful to rot." So, one bad tenant can cause a whole structure to lose its reputation and become a liability to the community and a reason for abandonment by the law-observing, good-housekeeping families that are exposed to these influences; a single landlord, bent upon "milking" his property, can damage a whole block front. These are some of the causes that must be simultaneously attacked if the wholesale abandonment that now plagues many close-in areas of central cities is to be checked and the social resource of old but solid structures is to be preserved.

It is to be noted carefully that a program of conservation that embraces an attack upon all these forces must

---

occupy; but that it represents a "solution" of this intricate and complex problem is a premise that is based upon the same oversimplification of the problem as that which permeated the previous proposals that have proved so disappointing in their realization.

be one that is conducted jointly by the private and the public sectors. And among the greater contributors to the success of such a coordinated program will be some of the landlords and housing managers who are conscientious in their operations but have been either ignored or viciously abused in many of the programs which have been supported by public funds, both local and Federal.

A program of governmental intervention in local housing markets that will attain the greatest public support and bring assistance to the greatest number of those who most need help with their housing problems will be one that works with the forces that operate in private markets, not against them; one that supplements rather than supplants the actions of private markets.

NOTES

1. Senator William E. Brock, in a speech before the Young Mortgage Bankers Conference of the National Mortgage Banking Conference, Atlanta, Georgia, April 4-5, 1972, reported in The Mortgage Banker (June 1972), p. 16.

2. In 1970, the FHA alone was administering more than 50 separate programs. HUD Statistical Yearbook, 1970, p. 148.

3. HUD Newsletter 2 (October 4, 1971) 36.

4. The distinction was pointed out in the Fourth Annual Report on National Housing Goals, forwarded by President Nixon June 29, 1972 (Washington, D.C.: Government Printing Office, 1972).

5. Quoted from the author's report to the Administrator of the HHFA on "Housing Policies and Programs," 1960, from which the rest of this topic is adapted.

ERNEST M. FISHER is professor (Emeritus) of urban
land economics at Columbia University in the City of New
York. He has been on the faculty of the University of
Wisconsin, the American University in Beirut, the University of Michigan, Rutgers University, and Columbia. He
has also worked in business: for the American Bankers
Association, the National Association of Real Estate
Boards, and the Federal Reserve System. He has served in
public office: in the Federal Housing Administration, and
as a consultant to the Bureau of the Budget, the Housing
and Home Finance Agency, the Department of State, the
Bureau of the Census, the Library of Congress, the Defense
Housing Coordinator, the Central Statistical Board, the
Central Housing Committee, the League of Nations, the De-
partment of Commerce, and to Congressional Committees.

Dr. Fisher is the author of <u>Principles of Real Estate
Practice</u>, <u>Advanced Principles of Real Estate Practice</u>,
<u>Home Mortgage Loan Manual</u>, <u>Home Mortgage Lending</u>, <u>Urban
Real Estate Markets: Characteristics and Financing</u>, <u>Urban
Real Estate</u>, and <u>The Mutual Mortgage Insurance Fund</u>. He
has also authored numerous articles which have appeared in
technical and professional journals.

FEDERAL GRANTS TO LOCAL GOVERNMENT:
An Analysis of Public Housing and
Urban Renewal
                    Richard D. Bingham

HOUSING THE POOR
                    edited by Donald J. Reeb
                    and James T. Kirk

MANDATORY HOUSING SUBSIDIES: A Comparative
International Analysis
                    Morris L. Sweet
                    and George Walters

RACIAL TRANSITION IN THE INNER SUBURB:
Studies of the St. Louis Area
                    Solomon Sutker and
                    Sara Smith Sutker

THE ECONOMICS OF RESIDENTIAL REHABILITATION:
Social Life of Housing in Harlem
                    Hyung C. Chung

URBAN HOUSING IN THE UNITED STATES:
A Crisis of Achievements
                    Charles J. Stokes and
                    Ernest M. Fisher